LOST BETWEEN THE CRACKS

THE TALE OF BEING HARDY

Liana—
enjoy reading the tale
of Mona's journey as you
prepare to begin a new
journey of your own ♡

MONA HARDY
SHAEMICHELLE WATSON

SW

Lost Between The Cracks

tellwell

Tellwell Talent
www.tellwell.ca

ISBN
978-0-2288-9642-5 (Hardcover)
978-0-2288-9641-8 (Paperback)
978-0-2288-9643-2 (eBook)

TABLE OF CONTENTS

DEDICATION

For Linda, for being there when others weren't.

For Max, and my niece, Zebrina,
who I will always love and are always there for me.

And for ShaeMichelle, for writing this book.

INTRODUCTION

This story is Mona's. This story belongs to her. This story will let you know her. For all my labour, it has nothing to do with me. Over the years I worked with Mona, I learned I needn't worry about inserting myself into the story; Mona is immutable.

When you meet Mona, you're first struck by her sense of fashion. She has a unique look about herself that is complemented beautifully with a seemingly endless collection of berets in every colour of the rainbow. She wears the berets perched on top of her salt-and-pitch-coloured hair. She usually wears neat, bright cardigans; her black and neutral cardigans have delicate and floral patterns. She always wears jewelry, usually gold or at least golden, sometimes adorned with crystals or diamonds. Her lips, like my grandmother's, are always painted in a deep berry or a true red. But Mona is, above all else, warm. She is welcoming.

She is a woman of her time.

Of course, Mona's look is the first thing you notice until you speak with her. From there, you're struck by her boisterous nature. She has a dedicated sense of humour and loves to laugh. But Mona is also bright. She speaks multiple languages: Anishinaabemowin, her first, then English, Polish and Ukrainian, French, and pieces of many more. Mona is incisive and brave. She stands out in a crowd. Her intelligence is blindly clear. She has a dignified aura, yet she doesn't intimidate.

For all my writing skill, I struggle to find another word than "boisterous" for her. She is full of life and she bubbles with an urge to invite you to enjoy life with her. She does this in spite of her trauma and the challenges of her life, or perhaps because of it. After all, she has overcome every challenge she has faced.

Mona is a deeply kind person and has spent much of her life advocating for others. She has many stories from her time as an advocate for the homeless. She made friends with bikers who would keep her safe when she was trying to persuade women to leave their violent pimps. So many of her stories are like that: facing danger and turning it to her benefit, or seeing suffering and finding solutions.

But Mona is not perfect, of course. She is crass in her own way, with firm and unshakeable opinions that she has no compunction about sharing. As Whitman and Dylan say, Mona contains "multitudes;" at times, she contradicts herself. She'll say she abhors violence but then talk about how much she wants to slap someone into silence or take revenge on behalf of a friend or cousin.

I met Mona in 2017. She has been a long-time patient of my nephrologist father's in the dialysis unit here in Thunder Bay, Ontario. Mona mentioned to him that she was trying to write an autobiography, but for all her brilliance, writing did not feel like her skill. She struggled to sew together her story in the same way she could skillfully sew moccasins or weave baskets. She is a storyteller, not a story writer. She bounces from one story to the next, always following the organic stream of her mind, especially as she ages. She has no ability to compartmentalize on paper and feels lost with a pen in her hand.

My father knew writing was in my blood. He'd read a constant flow of my short stories since I was young. I met Mona when I was an undergraduate working on my thesis, which turned into a multi-award-winning novel dealing with themes of trauma, recovery, identity, gender, and so much more. It was because of my love of writing that my father insisted I meet with Mona and offer to write her book.

I was hesitant at first; I didn't feel experienced enough as a writer and was unsure if I could do Mona justice. As I said before, I needn't have worried. Mona is immutable. While I spent many hours editing and reorganizing her thoughts, this book all comes from her. It's short because, in her advanced age, she remembers only the best parts. I also did not want to write extended sections based on her suffering. Even though she's experienced a multitudes of struggles, I wanted this to be a book of her joys, her strengths, the triumphs that will encourage others to seek the best parts of themselves.

I recently presented Mona with a draft of this book. As she read it, she wept at parts, laughed at parts and mused about how much life she had lived. Mona spends her time looking forward; looking back is not in her nature. Seeing her life in a summary seemed to engross her; she devoured the book in front of me, reading eagerly and only pausing to make sure she was keeping the unbound, double-sided pages in the right order as she turned them.

Chi-miigwetch for reading this book. This Anishinaabe phrase is used to mean thank you, but it literally means "that is very much enough" because "thank you" does not exist in Anishinaabemowin. Giving was a given. Sharing was a cultural norm. You might say, "miigwetch"—that's enough, that's sufficient—but there is no emotional load to it.

I owe it to Mona to do her story justice, and I hope my work is enough. I hope this book, short as it is, serves Mona's story well.

LEARNING THE HARD(Y) WAY

All that the wrongs that happened in my life were for a purpose: for me to learn the hard way, I guess.

What I remember about the lumber camp was everybody smelling bad. There was no personal hygiene. You had a whole bunch of people in a one-room shack; it could get very raunchy. There were no windows. There was just a door with a mosquito net on it.

All I remember is carrying water, looking after my younger siblings, sweeping floors. I must have been very young because we were there for a couple of years before we moved back to Macdiarmid, Ontario, where my brother Mervin started Indian day school and I started the year after.

There are a lot of working men in the camp. My father said none of them spoke English. They were all Finlanders.

And I guess that's my first recollection ever seeing a non-Native person. It would have been the Finlanders: men, loggers. Rugged and impersonal with the Aboriginals they worked amongst. At least impersonal with the Native children who ran about the lumber camp. I would see them when I had to go to the toilets. There were only two toilets, so that's where you would see the white men.

I also remember a lot of carrying water. It was not too bad in the summer, but in the winter, I had to chop a hole in the ice. I remember kneeling on the hard ice, breaking bits away with a pick and hauling water with a tin bucket that had cooled so much by the time I made it through the ice that it stung my skin with its cold.

I must have been about five years old. Sometimes I look back on the adults who let such a little kid chip ice and get angry. I think, *Hey, come on; do better.* But I guess that's why I was never lazy in my lifetime. Because I started off working, in a good and a bad way.

At the camp, I didn't like it that the four of us—my nearest siblings and I—we had to share this tiny little bed. If one of us peed or was sick, or if one of us couldn't soothe and stop crying, then it was me who was up all night. And I had a lot of chores in the daytime; I needed to sleep. God help me if my mother found me with a baby who had a dirty diaper. I felt like telling her, "This is *your* kid."

When we moved back to Macdiarmid, which is now Rocky Bay Reserve, we had a half-decent house. Two bedrooms upstairs, two downstairs, a humongous kitchen and dining room that could fit twenty people, with a dining room table my dad and grandfather made, with long, stately benches and everything.

By then I had learned how to cook on a wood stove and on an open fire. Sometimes big groups came over and I had made half of the meal.

But I was seven years old when I started school. So I must have been awfully young, caring for my siblings.

I don't know where my mother was. She didn't share her days with her children; I knew what some of my aunts were up to, but I never had a sense of where my mother was.

Maybe I avoided her, her dislike of me. Maybe that's why I don't remember.

She could have been working with my aunt, who was cooking at the camp for the men. Or she could have been visiting her sisters. Living right next to us was my cousin, Gertrude, and my aunts Esther and Jane in other cabins nearby. Gertrude and Moses: they were newlyweds, no children.

I don't ever recall seeing Esther and Jane's kids. But then again, I didn't see them because I was busy looking after my siblings inside.

I loved nurturing them, but I also wish I had had a childhood. I don't ever recall playing. I played with children in the house. But I played as a caretaker, not like a child.

I love children; I wish I had memories of really acting like one. Mainly I've always loved children. My biggest dream was to have a child, to bear a child. But then I found out that it was impossible.

My mother wasn't mean to me when my father was around. But when he wasn't, he'd been gone a week or three at a time. He worked in logging; they went off for weeks and then came back.

When he was at work, I would be beaten. It wasn't constant, but it was vicious when it happened. Even as a terrified child, shielding my head or face, I sometimes wondered what my mother's childhood was like, who had raised her that she could do this to me. Was she treated like she treated me? Did she think it was normal? Did she have a good childhood? Is this an anomaly? Is it my fault?

When you're little, you don't know any better. How can you?

When we moved back to Macdiarmid, my mother started getting mean because by then she could tell I was different.

I was different from day one. I was born odd, or at an odd time.

All of my siblings were born in winter, all but me. I was the only one born in June. I was different. They would say to me: "You're acting like a girl." But I was never acting. That was the problem; it was not an act. Nobody understood but my grandmother and my aunt.

My grandmother told me I was either born too late or too early. If I had been born earlier, there wouldn't have been any problem that I was a girl. Other people would have been more accepting. I would have had an important role, would have been seen as someone who the ancestors had made to bridge the gap between women and men, the past and the now, and the future.

And my aunt, if it weren't for her, I'd have been hungry a lot at the camp. My aunt always came by with food; I was always full because of her.

Back then, Macdiarmid wasn't even a reserve. We lived over in Macdiarmid; down the road, the Reserve was over there. Eventually, people were leaving as the fisheries were dying. As that fishing business died, as the people left, the reserve bought the properties, almost all of them. Now down at that end, there's two or three houses that belong to Greenstone and the reserve would not buy them. As long as they belonged to Greenstone, the Highway Department had to come down and plow.

I was a child; it was a good little town, Macdiarmid. It was one or two stores, the packing shed. Tourists would come and buy crafts and goods on their way through to bigger cities. We used to bleach flour bags, embroider them beautifully and sell them as pillowcases. I would embroider art on burlap sacks, too, using the brown as a simple background for little square embroidery scenes.

There was a little restaurant run by a Finn woman. We called her Dirty Gertie; she had the dirtiest apron ever. We weren't making fun of her; she was kind to us. She used to give a lot of us kids birthday parties.

She and her husband had no children. He worked in a bush camp, driving a truck. And she ran this little restaurant. I don't even think the restaurant made them money. She just gave so many things away. She had her husband build a stage outside for the kids to dance on. And she would put money in a jukebox for us just so we could make shows of nothing just for her, on her little stage. She was happy.

They say she made the best hamburgers anybody ever made. I don't know; I have never tasted them.

I loved it when my cousin Gertie would visit us. She would come and bring some tea and some bannock. She would always complain and ask why I was doing so much. I was only a child. It bothered her that we kids did so much work around the house; she thought we ought to be kids, spend time imitating adults instead of replacing them. She'd complain when my mother would send me out to chip ice.

My mother and Gertie were about the same age. I would visit Gertie every chance I got.

I loved going to my aunt Rose's home too. She was my mother's oldest sister. They named her Rosie because of her rosy cheeks. All the other sisters had biblical names like Mary, but they called her Rosie because of her cheeks. She carried those bright, smiling cheeks her whole life. She did her best to give other people smiles.

Oh, I had too much fun there. That's one of the only times I remember having fun. We made cookies, we made pies. She put on the gramophone and we would be dancing. She had two kids my age. We'd be dancing and we would play cards.

I look back on that time fondly.

My aunt Mary was another story. Nobody made fun of her. She had no kids. As an adult when I went to visit her, after I left home and I went back to visit, she told me she'd had a child when she was young. Something went wrong in birth; it was stillborn and she couldn't have another one.

I remember distinctly once, my aunt wanted to make me French fries. She sent me to the store and told me to come back with a bottle of ketchup, some bread, and Carnation milk for the kids.

There were some white kids there at the store, and they threw rocks at me when I came out of the store. I tried to run, but they hit me with some of the rocks. They hit the bag I carried with rocks.

They broke the ketchup bottle with a rock. It shattered and I heard that shatter louder than it actually was.

I went straight home from the shops. When my aunt saw me, she freaked out. She ran to me and she clutched me with her hands, panicked. She thought I was covered in blood. When I wasn't, she hugged me with relief and I felt very loved.

When I was small, I would go visiting my family when my dad was home. That's the only time it was freedom. But my father's work changed. Suddenly, he would be gone to work for four weeks, only coming back every fifth week. Without him around to hide her temper from, my mother got really mean. Really, really mean.

I asked her once, "What did I do wrong? I didn't ask to be born. I didn't ask to come into this world." She didn't answer my question. But I sure got a beating.

I was pretty clever as a child.

For one thing, I knew that it was wrong for grown-ups to be mean to kids, or to ignore us, or to not help us when we were scared. I knew it was even worse that my own mother didn't care to be kind or pay attention to us. I used to think, *How come nobody else knows what's happening here? It's not right.*

Even as a little kid, I never understood why I was the only one who acted like the bad stuff happening was wrong.

Maybe it was the norm in every household. Maybe no one noticed because they were too busy wondering why no one noticed what was happening to them. Maybe no one noticed because they were too busy keeping their own abuse a secret.

I had ideas of grandeur. You know, like, I didn't belong there. I should be somewhere else. Like, I lived in fantasy. I think that's what kept me going, almost like a form of meditation.

As a child, I started babysitting and instead of getting paid I used to babysit for clothes, toothbrushes, toothpaste. But eventually, I got a few dollars. I saved it all up, but it still ran out fast when I left.

When we were at the lumber camp, our father would bring branches home. He would bring us these big branches from pine trees and he would have us kids pick the pine cones. And we would sell them to Forest Services. That's where they got the seedlings for replanting back then.

My grandmother used the long pine needles to make baskets. I learned how to make baskets too. Last year, baskets I made I gave as a decoration for our new office. I like making baskets; I like the hard work of it. I like the challenge of working with the damp, in cool water that's no good for your hands. And when you're done the basket, you have a special gift to give away.

I was very young when I started school. I remember it was in Indian day school that I was introduced to drinking milk. The school supplied powdered milk and dog biscuits for us kids at the Indian day school. It was a one-room school up on the hill.

We had a teacher, a woman who was originally from Nipigon, and a single teacher's aide for all us kids. It wasn't enough to really teach us but was enough to occupy us in class day-to-day. After school, her aide would ask me to stay a while.

Her aide sexually abused me during those times I was held back.

Meanwhile my siblings went home and reported that I was being kept back; I must've been bad, I must be in detention. So when I got home, victimized, I got a beating from being bad in school.

I couldn't explain what was happening. They had no idea what was happening, other than pain. I want to make sure you understand: Grade 1 to Grade 13, all of us, in a one room shack. And with us all on top of one another, without enough textbooks or teachers or education between us, that aide still found a way to get me alone, to abuse me.

It took me a long time to finally complete the Indian day school application the Canadian government requires to compensate you for the abuse you suffered in their schools. Whatever "compensate" means when there's been abuse of a child. As if you can restore someone's childhood, their youth, their innocence.

I will get my compensation. It will not erase the pain of what I've gone through. I don't think it will make me any happier. I think it might help me move into a nicer building and might give me the financial comfort to give great gifts to those I love when holidays and birthdays come around. It might make me a bit more secure, financially.

But it doesn't erase the pain. It is compensation, not reconciliation. Reconciliation means action, not money. Reconciliation must be breathed by every Canadian or it will never happen. For a long time, I did not think my compensation would happen.

But here I am. Some say victim, some say survivor. I say I am Mona.

WHAT DOES IT MEAN TO HAVE A FAMILY?

My eldest sibling was stillborn and is still buried in Grand Bay, Ontario, a lonely, remote area on Lake Nipigon. Most of our elders are up there. They died before our community moved to Sand Point then to Macdiarmid now known as Biinjitiwaabik Zaaging Anishinaabek, or Rocky Bay.

The second born, Ray, who is a hard-working family-oriented man, married Linda and had four children. Like a lot of marriages, it came to an end in a battle for custody. My brother remarried Beatrice and both came to the end in an automobile accident. My parents became legal guardians of those kids.

The next child is Marvin, who died in childhood. The next in line was Ellis, who married Dolores and had four children. His second wife Donna had two daughters with him. Then came Ruth, the third wife, and they had two children. His last wife, Marlene, had one son. Ellis died of cancer, and not long after his oldest son Ellis Junior died of complications with asthma.

Then came Judy, who died when she was five years old. She convulsed and went into a coma, and she never came out of it.

Then came Ernest. He married my good friend Beverly. They both were teachers, and they had one son.

Then came Marjorie-Ann, who also went into convulsions and passed. My parents refused an autopsy then too; they said it was bad enough their girl had died. They didn't want her cut up.

Then came Mervin, who has fathered two children that I know of.

After that came Charles, who married Rolande and had four children. He died from liver cancer. Charles was one of my favourite siblings; he always had a warped sense of humour. When I lived far from home, he always provided me with airline tickets to come to Thunder Bay to visit or to go to funerals. He made sure I never missed out. It was so sad when I lost him.

After Charles came Theresa. She married a man called Frank, and they had three children.

Then came Cecile, who married Ernie. They shared one child together, while Cecile had a second child with someone called Herb.

Then came Geraldine who also convulsed. My sister was five years old, happy and doing the twist. She fell down and never got back up. She convulsed like my other siblings had, but she didn't die. The doctors decided she had had a stroke. She was only five years old. She came out of it, but she was paralyzed and blind. The Children's Hospital in Toronto told my parents, when they were taking her home all those years ago, that they were taking her home to die. That she'd only have a week, a month if she was a fighter. They told my parents they would never see her grow up. She is sixty years old now. She's still alive here in Thunder Bay; if it weren't for the pandemic, I would be seeing her often still.

But even before then, the pharmaceutical therapy she was given made her less and less able to speak. She became mute and immobile in the home. She used to scoot herself up the stairs, used to toilet herself, used to do all sorts of things in order to maintain her independence. She was mostly blind but could tell the food cans apart by feel. When she lived at home with my parents, she used to take the labels off the cans so she was the only one who knew what was inside, so the family would need her for a change.

It's been impossible to see her because of COVID-19. It's been impossible to try to argue with her caregivers, to see if fewer drugs would return the sister I used to know back to me. I worry sometimes that the time I have left with my sister will be interrupted by the pandemic completely.

Lastly was born Bryan, who was the best thing that happened in my childhood. His birth brought me so much joy. I nurtured him. I called him my baby. I made his formula; I changed his diapers during the night; I washed the diapers in the morning. My mom was suffering from post-partum depression. At first she wanted nothing to do with the child. Later in life, Bryan became her favourite too. It was one of the few things we had in common; we loved Bryan. Bryan married Jennifer when he grew older and they had one child.

I do believe that most of my siblings had to battle with their own demons, with drugs, with alcohol, with sexual abuse. Some became abusers themselves. Things that I advocated against my entire life exist within my own family.

Coming to terms with them can be an issue. There are things I know about our childhoods that some of them deny. I suppose it's easier than remembering. It's easier to deny than to really acknowledge what you went through, what you survived—and at the hands of people you loved, still love, still share blood with.

Let me not forget to mention my adoptive siblings, the children my parents adopted after I'd left home to live on the streets in white cities. There is Kalienda, who had one child. There is Wanita, who had one child. There is Robin, who married Amede and had two children. There is also Dalles Ray, who had five children, one of whom was stillborn.

My parents are first cousins. Their marriage was sort of arranged by the bishop. The bishop allowed them to get married because there wasn't nobody to marry. We were all one big happy family.

But I think that's why my sisters died. My father told me once he sometimes wondered if he had allowed an autopsy on his first lost daughter, if the doctors would have found something and been able to save the others. He wondered if it wasn't bad luck but a consequence of his genetics sabotaging them.

In our families on the reserve, there were a lot of child and baby deaths. If one could go to the older cemeteries, up at Grand Bay, one would find the majority of the graves were babies. A lot of the families had numerous childbirths but not many children. Not everyone survived. Things have changed since then because most pregnant mothers have access to good medical care, prenatal vitamins, so much care.

In the early days, life was hard for a lot of people. Those were the days when you needed money to make money. You couldn't fish in a little canoe to support your family anymore; you needed a big fishing boat. You needed money to buy a boat to get the fish to sell the fish to make more money. You needed money because you needed a car to go out of town, to find a job in the lumber camp to get more money, or to get to town to buy good food for your kids and to spend all your money. Money, money, money.

Before, people managed without money. They managed with community. They helped each other; they built together as a community. The first thing I noticed when I returned to Rocky Bay as an adult was the lack of community. The togetherness was missing. People were more concerned about "me, myself, and I."

Our reserve is a beautiful place on the shores of Lake Nipigon, surrounded by small mountains. It's grown so much since I was a child. There are so many more homes. There are more street names. There is even a multimillion-dollar water treatment plant; no one chips ice and hauls water like I did as a child anymore. When I was a child, we had coal oil lamps, or gas lamps if you had the money for one, and outhouses instead of interior toilets. I can still smell the smoky air that came with the warm light of a coal oil lamp.

And I remember the stars at night. Without light pollution, you could see the bend of the galactic equator, the clouds of light that shone at night that make up the exterior of our galaxy. You could see the Northern Lights dance like spirits in the sky.

But I also remember shivering together with my siblings at night when it was too cold to get out from under the blankets to use the slop pail let alone make it through the snow to the outhouses. I remember trying to hold my bladder on those nights; I remember when someone would fail and we'd all lay there in the wet hoping it would warm up soon.

I have so many siblings. I had cousins too.

My cousins and I would play during recess at school, and we would hold play weddings. I always wanted to be the bride, and my girl cousins let me take turns at the role. One of my cousins went on to marry Joseph, a boy we'd pretend married at school, for real. He laughed with me once, saying, "I don't know how many times you made me marry you on the school ground. You married Poncho twice. You married Gregory four times. I think you married me seven times." He's not my husband, but I'll know him 'til death do us part all the same.

It's funny the children who become part of your adult life; you have all of these silly memories between you and only serious times going forward. Those silly memories of playing bride at school are some of my only memories of playing at all.

It appears that I have a lot of family, but appearances can be deceiving. I really don't have a lot of connections to my family anymore; time has separated us so much that they feel more like acquaintances. I'll spend my Christmases alone, no family feast to prepare. Sometimes I don't cook at all. I'll put up a tree at home, but I don't really know what the Christmas spirit is.

When I think of family, I think of the friends I've made who have been there for me when I needed someone to share with and talk to.

Some of my siblings don't talk to me. It makes me sad. Some of the best parts of my life were in childhood, and those parts were almost always about my siblings. I do communicate with my siblings. Sometimes they do feel like strangers because of all the history and space and time between us. It's a terrible feeling to know that you have a lot of family while it seems that there is no one to reach out to. Anishinaabemowin doesn't really have a word that means "family" precisely the way English does. Wiidkagamanak is the closest word I can think of; it means "everyone in our circle."

The Hardy family is big, but I feel outside of its circle sometimes. It makes me thankful for my friends, for the found family I've chosen. It makes me thankful for the few good memories I have of our childhoods together; I treasure these, especially the memories after Bryan was born.

I remember so clearly when Bryan, my baby brother, was born. My mother had a terrible bout of post-partum and I looked after Bryan like he was my baby. But other parts of childhood were sad, and I'd left home by the time he was four. He remembers that part of his life, though, when we would have these lovely moments when it seemed like us kids were the only ones in the world.

The first child my mother had was a stillborn—born still because my grandmother beat her while she was pregnant. I can only imagine the pain of losing a baby, and my mother, who certainly felt that pain, forgot the suffering enough to mistreat her future children? How could she grieve one and mistreat another?

How could she have suffered such a consequence, being hit by her mother, and then turn around and hit her own kids?

I try to rationalize it as an adult, with my own life full of moments of fear and bad decisions, but I fail time and time again. Why not just leave? Escape somehow. Why continue the pattern? It wasn't just that she was a bad mother to her own kids, that sometimes-ill-fitted parents become pregnant.

As for myself, family doesn't mean anything to me anymore. It can be chosen; it can be lost; it simply is, without meaning, like the changing moon. I guess I was away too long. Like all the

Christmases I spend alone. With my family, I go through the motions but that spirit feels missing.

Sometimes everything my family was is what I worked to become the opposite of. I have family addicted to drugs and alcohol; I never dabbled for more than a night. I left anyone who beat me, and I never beat a lover of my own. I never raped anyone, like some of my siblings. I guess maybe that's why sometimes my family and I don't see eye to eye.

I've seen what alcohol can do. It tears up families. Lives ruined, kids separated, sent away from their siblings to grow up in families that aren't theirs.

Over the course of my life, I've seen that again and again. I've seen people overdose, seen people lose their lives to drugs in a real sense, not only that they lose their family and jobs and friends before they die. I even saw a roommate of mine overdose once. I didn't want to get involved. It's only gotten worse with time; more and more overdoses are on the news it seems.

I often ask myself what happened that my family pushed me away when I was sober and careful and kind. I felt pushed away by my family, further and further away the harder I tried to reunite. There were always insults saying that I was stupid, crazy, never around. I left because I was suffocating, but they felt abandoned.

Still to this day I get this backlash. I often think, *Why don't you look at yourself, your situation, and realize you're not better than me? I'm not better than you; I just dealt with my demons.* I stayed drug and alcohol free. I didn't need artificial stimulation to deal with being who I was. I made who I was someone I could live with sober. I didn't do things that would haunt me and make me need to drown bad memories; I chased my dreams and tried to build good memories around me. I didn't seek out distraction or salves from substance.

Being trans in the early days was hard enough without covering it up in artificial feelings and risking yourself and your mind with drugs. I saw it happen too often. Working trans girls, ones selling their bodies because they didn't know what else to do to survive, some would lean into drugs to cope with it.

More often than not, that made them the one the men who disappear people would choose. Being high or drunk and sloppy makes you a target for murderers and rapists and people who want to make sure trans people don't exist. Sobriety was my safety blanket. I didn't want to be like those disappeared women just as much as I didn't want to be an angry drunk who would beat their spouse.

It isn't only that I am transgender. After all, before colonialism, our traditional values would have had a place of honour for me. Being trans or two-spirited gave you a special connection to the Creator. That connection was destroyed by tricky treaties and residential schools and the pass system and mothers losing status when they married for love but married too pale a man.

It isn't only that I'm transgressive in the modern sense that some of my siblings exclude me from their lives. Even when we were small, I read everything, everything was different. I see everything wrong in my family's view.

I never understood how you could beat someone you claimed to love, but so many people in my family are so used to it that they accept it. I've seen that when babysitting for my cousin Fred. He used to beat up his wife Mary. She'd be black and blue. Holy shit, if you could've seen what he'd do to her. Eventually she left him. But eventually can be a long time.

My cousin Violet was beautiful but married a drunk who beat her. He beat her so bad her face became deformed over time, shaped into asymmetry by his fists, making her ugly to anyone but him.

I guess my dad drank a drink, but he wasn't a chronic drunk, at least not that I remember. My mother didn't drink at all, not while we were little. I think there was a period of her life after I left where she would go out and drink. I guess most of us were grown up by then.

I learned a lot in those first years at school. I was around other kids than my siblings for the first time; I wasn't a primary caretaker at school, just another Indian kid shoved in front of the nuns.

From my cousin, I learned what it meant to run away. She had a sense of what was happening to me and she said, "We should run away." It was the first I'd even heard of the idea that I could leave the environment I was in or that one day I would. But we were much too young then to run away.

I eventually would when I was older. It took time to get used to the idea of leaving. It took a long time to get used to the idea I could find something better. It took even longer to find it.

When I was a child in school, I was good at sports. I could outrun anybody. I outjumped everyone. I was even good on the balance beam.

But I never made it all the way through school. I hit a wall in Grade 9 and that was as far as I got. In Grade 9, other people started noticing how different I was. For one, most of the students were white.

So I hid most of the time. I could tell that the nurse felt sorry for me, so she would send me to a sick room almost every day. She could tell I was sick of the abuse. She knew I stood out amongst my peers, how they made fun of me for my girlish ways and my darker skin; she knew, too, that it must not be much easier for me at home from the way I would talk about it when she got answers out of me. I told her, eventually, how much I had wanted school to be a break from all that was going on at home.

But I'm surprised she never made a complaint. Nowadays, when I work with people, especially children, and I suspect abuse? Nowadays, you have no choice but to make a report. You have to mitigate what's happening; there's no world in which you don't protect a child.

But policies didn't exist back then, and so children fell through the cracks.

I fell so far through the cracks that I left school. I fell so far through the cracks that I left home. I didn't finish Grade 9; I didn't stay where my mother's meanness could reach me. I went to Thunder Bay, Ontario, and stayed at my aunt's for a while. And when I was living with her, I realized it would be a long time before I felt like going home. That's when I decided it was time to get out of there.

I had no idea where I was going to go, just that I wouldn't go home. I went to the little trainyard in Thunder Bay and I climbed onto a freight train. Of course, at the time I didn't think it was a little train yard. I thought Thunder Bay was a big city then, even when it was two smaller cities with different names. The train stopped in Nipigon and it stopped in Sault Ste. Marie. I only knew I was heading east. Fourteen-year-olds don't think that far ahead; I only knew I was heading east.

LOVE AND LOSS IN TORONTO AND BEYOND

Then the train stopped in Toronto.

It seemed like the trainyard alone was bigger than the village where I'd grown up, let alone the brick and concrete city that rose up around it.

Toronto was terrifying.

There were more people than I'd ever seen in my life, all hustling and bustling to places and business and jobs I'd never heard of.

I'd been taught most of my life in Ojibwe, the same language I spoke at home, so my English wasn't very strong. I was frightened by the crowds; I couldn't enter the subway for the longest time because it seemed like more people got into a single car down there than we had in my whole village. Surely my entire self would get swallowed up in the crowd and I would lose me. What else would I have if I lost me? I was all I had.

I lived on the streets at first. I slept under stairways or in doorways.

I would make flowers out of paper I dug out of the trash and would sell those instead of begging. Some people were even generous when they bought them, like they saw how I was trying to earn my way instead of begging for it. Some people weren't so generous, like they saw no difference between someone lying useless in the gutter and someone trying to climb out.

I was maybe fifteen years old at a CNE—The Canadian National Exhibition—in Toronto, and there was a contest to see who could cook the best bannock.

I cooked my bannock on an open fire. I won fifty bucks, which was a lot of money those days. Some people asked me where I learned to cook on an open fire, and I said, "In the bush. You learn a lot in the bush."

Real life happens in the bush; it's not untouched wilderness. It's the home of so many people.

I went to Toronto, but eventually, I came back to Thunder Bay, seeking the warmth of a house and the welcome of family. I stayed with my cousin Barney and his wife. She was working at a nursing home and she got me a job in the kitchen. I worked there for maybe a year, a year and a half.

And then I went back to Toronto. Nothing was holding me to Thunder Bay, and there was more verbal abuse and all that in the streets of a small town than in the big city.

The first time I heard powwow drums I was on the streets of Toronto.

I couldn't believe it. I'd heard so much about powwows and now there were drums, here in the city, for me to experience. I rushed through the streets towards the sound. I could feel the energy of the crowd. It was like nothing else.

But it turned out the drums belonged to Krishna devotees dressed in orange. The wrong kind of Indian drum.

Because we never heard of powwow as children. Like, come on people, nothing is real. Powwows are done for money. Nothing sacred about them. The regalia is not real. So much of our traditions are lost to time because of residential schools and all that; I think the regalia of today is made because it looks like the regalia white people made up in their movies, in Hollywood, when they'd hire Natives and put fake subtitles under what they were saying.

And I argue with people. It's all tradition being made up by us now; if you are Anishinaabe and make it, it is traditionally made. That's all there is to it.

I feel strongly about this. When I go to a ceremony or go someplace to teach or give a talk, women kept telling me again and again and again: I have to have a ribbon skirt. So I took my flamenco skirt and put ribbons on it. I sewed ribbons onto my flamenco skirt the same way you sew ribbons onto ribbon skirts. And I got snapped at—told, "That's not traditional."

I said, "Neither is yours. There's no such thing as a traditional ribbon skirt. Yeah, we did not have ribbons. Yeah, we did not have this fabric, not until the Europeans brought it to trade with us for squash seeds and furs."

All this regalia. Ribbons come from Europeans; we made up this tradition when Ukrainian loggers and Finnish loggers and whoever else traded crafting materials with us for our own goods.

What makes it traditional is us. We are the only tradition; what we see as our art becomes our traditional art. What we make is real.

The rest is made up.

Everything is made up, it seems, even our empathy as a society. I am writing this section while the war rages in Ukraine because one insane old man started a fight he can't win. And everyone is feeling badly for Ukraine. Everyone is sharing photos of children and refugees running from the war and everyone is having an outpouring of grief about it.

But there are wars all the time. There have been wars raging in Africa and no one has been outpouring their grief down to them. Israel does to Palestine what Russia is doing to Donbas; no one in the West ever acts like it is the same, but it is.

It makes me think this all comes down to racism. It's a white country being invaded and that seems unnatural to white people; they think it's natural that brown and black people have war, but not them. We make up our empathy when it suits our made-up hatred.

There's a lot of made-up hatred for trans people. We exist the way we do because it's how the Creator made us. We live our lives moving between the ends of the spectrum of gender that most people pin themselves to.

I think that scares people: the idea that they define themselves in a cultural gender just as much as we do; they just don't get to experience the freedom and struggle of defining that cultural role for themselves.

Some say God created man and woman, nothing else, not trans people. Some say if we change ourselves to live our truth, we're changing what God gave us. They say that's wrong.

But God, the Creator—whoever—he gave us lots of things we are meant to change. He gave us grain but not bread. He gave us grapes but not wine. We add yeast to both things; we change them with the power of life and make them suit our own purposes.

Being trans is just the same: you add life to what you were given and become your true self. But with made-up hatreds, it can be a rough path to walk. A rough way to live.

The big city of Toronto was rough for other reasons, that was true.

It wasn't very welcoming to the trans community, for one thing. So many trans people lived in poverty, and many were forced into prostitution.

A lot of trans folks got a good education, trying to get out of poverty with the promised path of school, only to find out how hesitant people were to hire people like us. Some trans women are never read as women; people see them and see a man trying to be something he's not—but she *is* what she is. *She is.*

"She is" is a complete sentence, but it's one that makes people uneasy; it makes them shut us out. Life is not fair to some, while others excel.

There were many accepting individuals in Toronto, but the system was not friendly to any kind of queer person. There were police raids on the clubs we knew as gay bars. They could arrest you just for being there or could take your money from your wallet while checking your ID.

The trans community wasn't even allowed out until after dark; dressing in clothes other than the gender you were assigned at birth met the criminal definition of legal indecency. You were only allowed to do it at night, like you were a creature of lore: a vampire, not a person.

I met a lot of working girls who only worked to support their drug habits; I mean, I knew them at their lowest points in their lives. These girls were there like me: not because they wanted to be but because they saw no other way to escape from the trauma of their youth. Some were so abused as little girls they just wanted to forget. They accepted sex work as the only kind of affection they could get. Some committed suicide; more overdosed.

I thank my lucky stars that I never got hooked on drugs. It saved me perhaps more than anything else. But I learned one should not criticize the other people; you don't know their history or what abusive situation they're escaping or what anguish they feel.

So many trans folk like me were forced into prostitution because their bodies would sell when their honest labour wouldn't.

And sometimes cops would bust them up for being prostitutes but would let them go after a blow job. The cop would arrest you for sex work and make you do sex work to earn your freedom again. There was no justice; there was only the fact that trans folk, women especially, were lesser and cops were powerful. I know this because I did what I had to do to survive, especially in the winters.

Canadian winters are harsh.

Winters here are cold. The very air turns to vicious wind, seeking wind that bites you. Unlike in the bush, you can't dig a well in the snow to start a fire and hide from the wind. You can crouch in alleys and stoops and try to sleep over subway grates, but people will chase you away. In the bush, you can pitch a camp anywhere. In the city, there is nowhere to be if you don't have money to pay. Merely existing without spending money is loitering; they can charge you with the crime of existing without spending money.

Canadian winters in the city are harsher than trading sex for a cheap room to avoid freezing to death. They are harsher than letting a stranger use you like a tool.

I understand desperation. I used to trade sex for a room for the night or for supper. A man, kind in his own way, pointed out that I should start selling myself for money instead so I could rent a room and eat when and what I liked. It made sense so I tried to carve out a home for myself that way. I told myself it was always going to be temporary.

Temporary can be a long time.

I'm a professional now, and I present myself professionally. Sometimes the vulnerable people I work with tell me that I can't possibly know what it's like to be poor. In those professional settings, I just can't blurt out my past. I can't blurt out what dignity of mine was stolen by police, by men on trains and in motels, by the innumerable abusers I knew when I was in poorer shoes.

Working the street isn't a profession that I would recommend. It's dangerous. There are a lot of quacks out there who will not think twice about robbing or violating you. But on the other hand, there are a lot of sad, lonely men who can't commit to normal relationships.

Being a hooker doesn't always mean sex. Some men just want company and they are too bizarre or sad or angry to find it anywhere else. In my later years of trading myself this way, I had a lot of gay professionals hire me to escort them to plays, operas, concerts and to family weddings. I was often told I don't have the makings of "other working girls." I guess I would pick and choose my clients.

Sure, I was desperate and homeless, but I wasn't on drugs. The desperation of drugs is different. I still had some choices.

But in my younger years, I learned a lot from that desperation before I met the love of my life.

His name was Eric.

Eric was a handsome man from Portugal with the muscly build that came from hard honest work. He did that hard work and kept his soft eyes, his kind smile, a gentle touch.

We met when I was on the street in the wintertime. I was still a teenager.

Eric saw me on the street, sitting in the snow with no place to go, and he took me in. He gave me a place to live and seemed to expect nothing but conversation. His home had thick, luxurious blue shag rugs and a sunken living room. It was luxury like I'd never known. I was a little homeless youth, but he invited me in and didn't worry that I'd ruin the thick shag with the feet I'd be living on. He made me feel at home.

Eventually, we developed a relationship. He would go to work as a cabinet maker and I would have dinner ready when he got home. He gave me a room in his apartment with no strings attached, but he was so kind. He restored my faith in humanity, my trust in humankind. I couldn't help but fall in love with him. Soon he was in love with me too.

Eric worked as a cabinetmaker back when custom cabinetry meant much more than plywood boxes cut to exact sizes. He did the intricate, delicate, lovely woodwork finishing on custom cabinets. He'd carve concentric circles and whorls and other beautiful shapes into storage, turning utilitarian storage into art. Sometimes he'd take me to his work at night so we could spend time together even if he had to finish a project. It was always so impressive watching him work.

He was strong from lifting solid wood doors and cabinet units, but he also had the ability to carve delicate, beautiful designs into the heavy, quality wood. They don't even make cabinets like that anymore; people don't respect labour enough to pay for hand-cut, unique, traditional designs like that. Nowadays even custom cabinets are minimalist, so simple to be boring. What Eric made was art; it brought art and culture into kitchens, into homes.

One time when we'd been together about three years, we went to Centre Island to watch the fireworks. We had a nice time; we had hot dogs at the little fairground there. After the fireworks, late at night, we took the ferry back to the city. We decided to walk home, caught up in the evening and never wanting it to end.

It had been such a perfect night.

We began our wander through the dark, night-time streets. Our shoulders would bump and our laughter would echo off the buildings around us. There is an unforgettable quality to being in love; Eric was unforgettable.

We lived between Dundas West and Lansdowne, on Bloor. It was on the way home from Centre Island that lovely night with fireworks that everything changed.

A bunch of men overcame us.

We hadn't done nothing to them. They didn't even seem to be robbing us; it seemed more vicious and motiveless.

It felt like hate.

Eric was beaten to death and I was raped.

It was a senseless crime. It lasted forever, and when they left us in the gutter, I realized how bad it had been. I realized, while I lay bleeding, that Eric was not bleeding. Eric was not breathing.

Eric was dead.

Eventually, other pedestrians came upon us and called the police.

The worst part, after it happened … after I was raped by those men, after they beat Eric to death, after someone stumbled upon our bodies and called the cops. After the cops came. After the questions and the sirens and the flashing lights. After they photographed his body like an object, a piece of evidence to a crime they didn't seem to care about.

After the cops came, they picked up Eric's body. They put Eric in a bag. They put the bag in a van. They drove the love of my life away.

And then they left me there on the sidewalk.

The police left me there on the sidewalk, bloody and with ripped clothes. They took the body of the love of my life and I was left behind.

Police are people you're supposed to be able to trust, who are meant to be sworn to protect every citizen they see.

Instead, they left me there like something worthy of less dignity than a dog. Even a dog, they wouldn't have left there.

If they'd found a murder victim and his dog, they would have taken a dog to a shelter.

A dog shelter would make room. But me? The cops left me behind. They didn't take me to a shelter. A shelter might have turned me away.

After Eric was murdered, his body was sent home to Portugal, away from me, away from our home, away from the people who killed him and raped me and got away with all of it. No fanfare. No funeral, no service. Not here, anyway, and it wasn't as if I was in any shape to go to a service anyway.

That night on Centre Island was the last time I saw Eric. I try to remember his smile, his face turned up to the sky as the fireworks danced. I try not to remember the bag zipping shut over his broken face or the sound of the van door closing on the gurney they used to carry him.

After Eric was murdered, after he was beaten to death, I never wanted to get into another relationship. I was scared that it would happen again. It was so awful to lose someone so precious, so important. I didn't think I was strong enough to survive it again: not the beating, but the broken heart. The grief. The loneliness of waking up alone after hundreds of nights waking up with a beautiful, kind man with strong hands and precise eyes.

Once, years, maybe even decades later, I was at a group dinner and a former cop sat next to me.

I said to him, "I'm sorry, but I really don't like cops. I'd prefer it if you sat somewhere else."

He looked at me calmly. He asked why and I told him what they did to me when Eric was beaten to death. He admitted that even he wouldn't like cops if that had happened to him, and he did move on to sit somewhere else.

But me? I sit forever with Eric's memory.

Losing him changed me. I've loved since, but it is never the same. It's never like what loving him was like. He was the love of my life.

I really think we get one shot at true love. Even now, now that I'm old enough to write my memoirs, there isn't a day I don't think of him. In that way, he never really left me. His memory stayed with me and kept me going through so much. It made me who I am today.

When Eric died, my name wasn't on the lease of our apartment. I'd made a home in the shelter he gave me after all. We'd never gone out and shopped around for a new place to build a happily ever after. We thought we could do it in the place he already had when he found me. It would never have occurred to us he would be murdered like he had been. How could you plan for such a tragedy?

I couldn't even convince the landlord to let me in to get my stuff.

I ended up homeless, without any of my stuff. It was like I had time-travelled to a time before I knew Eric when he died: suddenly I had nothing again, not even him. I had none of our photos, none of our memories, nothing.

MOVING ON (OR LIVING WITH GHOSTS)

I did what I had to do to survive then. I slept in countless public washrooms to avoid the cold; I'd freshen myself up in the sink when I woke. Homeless and penniless on the street is the most undesired feeling. You barely have yourself; other than that, you have nothing.

People don't realise how lucky they are to have a home, a roof over their head, away from the extremes like the wind, rain and snow. Exposure strips you of humanity. You enter stores to try to warm up and they follow you and hover like you're going to steal.

I would go through garbage cans to find food. I used to find potato skins and bits of steak. Sometimes I'd have to scare off the cats or the raccoons to get that food. Sometimes I'd go where the cats were because they could smell what I couldn't.

Eventually, a dishwasher noticed I was going through a restaurant's trash. I thought, *Oh, this'll be the end of it. The dishwasher'll chase me off next time he sees me.* But I risked going back the next night and I found he had no intention of chasing me off.

Unbelievably, he had noticed me and seen me as a full person, fully human. He saw that I was real. Instead of protecting his boss's dumpster, he realized I was hungry. Instead of seeing a homeless animal going through trash, he saw a hungry girl. I was just a girl.

So he had taken some *good* food and he had put it in an actual takeaway box. He'd tucked the box on the ledge of the building's foundation for me, above the dumpster, dry and safe from cats and rats and roaches. He put *real* food in a *real* box, with a *napkin*, like I had ordered room service in a hotel. It was so special to me. It made me feel like a person again.

The next time he saw me eating from his garbage, from the takeout container he had made for me, I thanked him. I told him that he had a good heart. "God bless you," I said. I'm not really religious, but there is sometimes no bigger word for thank you than to ask something as big as God for a blessing.

It wasn't long after Eric died that a Polish couple took me in. I earned the kindness because they were surprised I could speak Polish. I, of course, had learned working in a hospital in Thunder Bay; everyone who worked in the hospital kitchen there was Ukrainian or Polish.

I learned little bits of vocabulary here and there, enough to be understood. The Polish couple had a lot of their relatives in Thunder Bay; they knew the streets I used to live on there.

Magda and Andrew lived on Pecumpsie, just off King Street. I stayed with them while I healed up, but we all knew I couldn't stay long or I'd become a burden. Magda worked in the King Hotel on King Street, so she stuck her neck out and got me a job in the dish room. I worked for a bit of a salary, a room in the hotel and one staff meal a day.

One meal was okay because I was obviously the dishwasher. I separated all the best scraps from the plates before I cleaned them. I would say it was for my dog, but really it was for me.

Lacking education, you work minimum wage. That's all anyone will give you: the bare minimum. There was not enough money to rent a decent place. So what is a girl to do?

I supplemented my income with men's money on the streets. I worked the streets two or three nights a week. Got myself a small bachelor apartment in a little complex on Lansdowne, living with cockroaches as roommates. I mixed in with the other tenants. I didn't feel so visible. Slowly, slowly, slowly, I began to feel safe; long after the bruises from Eric's murder had left me, the fear began to move into the back of my awareness too.

I got bold enough to take a client who was a member of parliament from Thunder Bay. He used to be a client of sorts of my father, and an uncle; when they worked as traditional hunting and fishing guides, he was one of the many settler men who would come in the summers to be paddled around and shown the best spots to catch walleye and pike and whitefish.

Even though he was an MP, he was well-known for listening to us Aboriginal folk, for listening to our issues and desires. If he hadn't died so young, he would have made so many good changes on our behalf.

He made good changes on my behalf, while I knew him. He was the one who found me the job at the Ontario Club.

The Ontario Club was an exclusive club. Employees had to enter through the back because this place was so fancy that the servants weren't allowed to use the same doors as the guests. There was a big divide between the workers and the guests, but that was OK. I still was treated well there. I learned a lot.

Some nights I would work so late I saw no point in making the commute to the bachelor studio I'd rented. It became more like a storage locker for the new memories and things I'd become to collect. I'd loiter and snooze in the kitchen's dry storage and the baker would say to me, "If you're gonna hang around here, you may as well do something."

One day, he forced me awake and he gave me an empty cake pan, flipped it over and gave me a bag of icing. I would decorate the cake pan as if it were a cake, and he would critique it, wipe off the icing and make me start again.

Eventually, after dozens of nights of practising with Russian buttercream and ermine frosting and whipped cream and fondant, I had satisfied him. After so much practice that I'd made perfect, he let me decorate the real pastries. I learned a lot at the Ontario Club. You can learn anything anywhere; all it takes is someone willing to teach.

I was only about seventeen or so when I worked there. It was one of my first real jobs in Toronto.

The Ontario Club had a buffet filled with more food and fancier food than I'd ever imagined before. And this chef could carve a turkey, put it back together and glaze it. It was a work of precision. It was a masterpiece, barely looking like it had ever been carved at all; the marvellous labour that made it possible was so well done as to be invisible. And guests could come to the reassembled turkey and simply take their piece.

They had whole smoked salmon with olives for eyes, and ice sculptures, and cocktails and caviar. I even got to try some caviar when I worked there. It was a very good place to work in my day.

The salad room for the guests was incredibly fancy. You would lay smoked salmon over a piece of lettuce, put a little bit of capers or pickled herring, all sorts of appetizers.

That was the year the K-Tel Salad Queen came out. It was an upright mandolin with a crank so you could slice or grate or julienne or whatever else the blade accessories could do just by turning. Perfectly prepared veggies came out. K-Tel or not, everything I prepped was perfect; they used to call *me* the Salad Queen.

But I worked all over that kitchen. I worked in the dish pit, on the line in the kitchen, in the bakeshop. In the bakeshop, I used to make these peanut butter cups, back when Reese's wasn't so popular, back when it would still be a novel candy for most people. I often say I invented them.

The Ontario Club was a very exclusive club. Workers there didn't get tipped out; you got a bonus every three months.

With the steady work, I started looking better.

I was out of the cold. I had a place to live.

It was then that I really started dressing as a young lady. The waitresses brought me their old clothes and I started wearing skirts and nice tops. I developed my own sense of style, not an outfit designed to keep me warm on the streets but to look like myself, to look like Mona Hardy.

I also did a lot of volunteer work. I volunteered at for the opera doing research for props from different eras. I fixed old, raggedy, stinky costumes and tacky old wigs I should have shown in the garbage.

By that time, I was perfecting my English. I'd already spoken some at home and when I'd lived with Eric, but it was around this time I became fluent.

One of my jobs was in a sewing factory. There was a mélange of languages spoken there, but it took me a long time to realize that. I suddenly doubted my fluency in English; surely I wasn't as skilled as I thought and that was why I couldn't understand the mix of words around me.

Eventually, I realized it was a jumble of something that I couldn't make out. The better I got at English, the more I could tell it apart from anything else. It was all Greek to me, as they say, and it turned out that some of the jumble I learned from was Greek.

When you're young and inquisitive (nosy is the word), you want to know everything. That's how you learn, eh?

Any time I was around something new, I had to know how it worked, why it worked like that. If I found a job and they showed me it should be done one way, I'd try to find a way to do it faster, be more productive. To make every task as easy as it can be isn't laziness; it's productivity.

That's why, when I was older, I got a job in education and found myself really enjoying the work I did with special needs students. There's no one way to do that job; there are only people who are good at it and people who aren't. When designing Individual Education Plans, you have to know not only what tasks the kid needs to do differently, but what part of the task they're stuck on. You need to know how to make their tasks easier.

But with a paycheque and a steady room and my own clothes, I let my pitch-black hair grow out past my knees.

I had flawless skin, the beauty of youth. I used to wear the girliest clothes then too. I wore microminis to show off my shapely legs. I had my long hair but no beard, no stubble. My hair was like a crown it was so shiny. But I didn't go out too much, so for all I knew I looked good. I was afraid of the outside world, I think.

I avoided abuse. I stayed put. I didn't go out. I almost made myself into a hermit.

Some of being a hermit wasn't my fault; sometimes I just didn't feel like taking the risk of being a person out in the open instead of being a thing that hides away. In those days in Toronto, if you were born and seen as a boy, you couldn't dress like a woman until *after* dark. That was the law. But I was young and beautiful, and I looked perfectly girly with my long hair and smooth face. Nobody noticed I was breaking the law. Still, it was a risk.

Knowing I looked like a girl didn't make breaking the law less scary. It wouldn't make me any safer that I looked nice in a skirt if I were arrested or if something happened to me and the cops didn't care. In some ways, it created its own kind of danger. Someone might decide to attack me because I looked like an Aboriginal girl, an easy target; if they realized who they really attacked, maybe they'd kill me too.

But staying in made me save my money. And eventually, I saved enough that I started living in fantasy again, like I did as a child in Macdiarmid. What was there to hold me down? The love of my life was gone. I had recovered from my physical wounds. I had the tiniest bit of savings.

So I left Toronto, a city filled with memories and a ghost, and headed to a new world. First, I went to Winnipeg.

DREAMING AND DANCING

While in Winnipeg, I met the first famous Aboriginal male ballet dancer, René Highway. His brother is the playwright Tomson Highway. They both left their Cree reserve like me, but they pursued art and succeeded in a way I hadn't yet. Meeting René inspired me. It made me relive my fantasies from when I was a child. Living in fantasy, I revived my dreams of being a dancer.

I ended up moving to New York to study contemporary dance and performance. In those days, you could just show up, no jumping through hoops for visas or work permits. I was, as they said then, a North American Indian, so I had citizenships on both sides of the borders the settlers made.

I was in my twenties by then, and ready for a taste of something new. Foolishly, I thought New York, farther south, would be warmer in the winter. But even the bustle of that city doesn't disguise the cold of winters on Turtle Island.

Of course, that changed after 9/11, when the whole world changed not because Americans died but because some of their most famous buildings were attacked.

Americans are in love with their buildings, their lines, their borders. They worship their buildings, and when one was destroyed the whole world changed. American Indians now live by the settler boarders; we need visas and work permits and passports to visit the land stolen from us.

The change didn't happen because of American lives; it was because of the buildings, an attack on the land they stole. After all, it became commonplace during COVID-19 for three thousand Americans to die in a day and the world kept turning. But not after 9/11. Not after those monuments to trade and money came crashing down.

I began classes at the Martha Graham School of Dance. Classes were from 5:30 a.m. to 8:30 a.m. or 1:00 to 4:00 p.m. at 55 Peter Street. I studied contemporary dance, a combination of jazz and lyrical and classical ballet. It wasn't easy like I thought it would be; I had dancing in my heart but it took a lot of study and discipline and vigorous exercise to bring it into my muscle memory.

There were so many starving artists; I worked many jobs to keep myself well fed. I worked in cafés and restaurants as a server. I worked as a dishwasher at one of the places; they gave me a salary and a free meal with each shift.

The place was very New York; it never slept, and the owner gave me the flexibility to work early mornings or late nights or busy lunches as my classes demanded. The mornings were the busiest. New Yorkers love morning takeout: café au lait, espresso, croissants, brioche, plain bagels ... so many bagels.

Sometimes I'd wonder if New Yorkers had toasters in their homes because they would pay so much for a toasted and cream-cheesed bagel that they could get for less than a dollar at home. But they wanted the greasy wax paper bag and the hot bagel as they wandered the streets packed with others. They paid for the privilege.

There were days I would fill in for the prep cook. I'd prep soups and set up the café with fresh tablecloths and flowers. I learned to make the little French pastries the morning takeout goers went crazy for. I always had the ambition to learn and was always eager to try new things. The sky was the limit whether in the café kitchen or the dance school.

Trying new things, practicing new skills, learning to be excellent at them made me think about my childhood, coming from the lumber camp with no encouragement and a constant reminder that people like me never amounted to anything. It was like my mother thought I was part of the rocky soil in Rocky Bay: ill-suited to growing anything that could sustain a good life. Maybe my eagerness came from wanting to one day prove her wrong.

I learned all I could studying, and I ended up working at the St. Mary's Club in New York. It was a trans club, a drag club, and a great place for dancing.

I managed to write two numbers—choreographed numbers—and I performed three shows a day for a couple of months. The first was called "Satan's Road to Hell," about the life of the transgender woman. No matter which way she walked, the walk would be hell. If she walked as she was born, as a boy, she had to *live* through hell. And to be able to walk as a woman, you have to *go* through hell. And at the end of my dance, a ring of fire would appear on the stage and I would drop to the floor. I would go to hell.

And the crowd would go *wild* for me.

The second dance I became known for was called "Every Man Should Be on a Leash." I was inspired by some bikers I knew in New York. Oh, they were fun, wild, unpredictable people. They made you want to put them on a leash just so you could control the party a little bit. To make the dance a spectacle like they were, I would show up on stage on a motorcycle with a man in leather on a leash.

It connected me with all the trans groups, girls too wild for me to keep up with. I never ran into other people who can be piss-eyed drunk and function normally like these girls. No amount of substances slowed them down. It did make me wonder sometimes, why bother with the substances? Why get piss drunk and spend the money if it didn't change how you acted?

New York wasn't bad. New York was bustle and life.

People hustled and bustled so much they wouldn't see you. You were invisible in a city that demanded uniqueness to make a living. No one could see you past the crowds and the noise. Everyone just went about their own business, trying to carve their own uniqueness enough to be seen. And while we all tried to do that, we rarely saw each other. We hustled and bustled.

I had a good life in New York. A good night life, especially. I would dance and club and party and dance some more. I think I stayed safe through it all because I never did drugs. I think that saved me. I guess you could say I was high on life. High on the bustle of New York.

I lived above a factory in the garment district with five other starving artists. We all had our own little tents on what used to be a manufacturing floor, and the floor had two showers and two toilets. We also shared a kitchen. Your privacy was in your little tents.

The lack of privacy fed into your creativity. There was always noise, always movement, always inspiration, always something going on. Even though I was a dancer, I wrote a play.

It was about a young girl leaving a reservation. She wanted to be an actress, like so many in New York and so many in the factory loft where I lived. But this girl came from the reservation, and she faced nothing but rejection after rejection. She got into alcohol to deal with it, got into the wrong people, got into drugs, got into jail.

In jail, she overdosed because she wanted to go home so badly. One of the performance teachers contacted Buffy Sainte-Marie and asked if we could use her song "Coming Home," which was the perfect song for the end of the play.

In the end, after she'd overdosed and died in jail, a chieftain with wings came down and took her up, up, took her up to go home with her mother. There was never a dry eye in the house.

But there were so many people studying these classic arts, and we all knew the chances of succeeding were so slim. We had to be better than the best, be one in a hundred—one in a million—just to succeed. When we started, we all thought we could be good enough to be that best one.

I realized it probably wasn't going to be me. After all, I couldn't do the dances I was doing forever. I couldn't survive off one very sad, very good play.

So I was smart enough to realize this. My dance show did a month-long tour, and that was enough for me. The dance and the crazy schedule was not the problem. I just knew there was so much competition that my chances to do anything else were so small. I didn't blend in or fit in enough to be successful, and I didn't stand out enough to get noticed.

New York was not home, no matter how good of a night life I had, no matter how much of an experience it was. And it was quite the experience.

As a trans dancer at a club, I had to deal with men who came in just to abuse us, just to be nasty. They'd call us a pervert or a psycho or some other insult and I'd just think, *You're the one who* paid *to get in here. You* waited in line *to pay to get in here. What does that make you?*

There's no place like New York. But it was no place for me.

Back in Toronto, I found a job at Runnymede Hospital as a dishwasher, and I worked my way up to prep cook. It was partially my hard work and my good ethics, but partially that I never stopped asking for a promotion. I was there for a couple of years. On summer holidays, I would replace the cook.

That's when I met a man whom I became wildly infatuated with. We started sleeping together, and then living together, and I started to think, *Wow, maybe we're in love.* But. But.

Twice he got drunk and twice he beat me. The third time, I said no.

I left my own home because of abuse, left MacDiarmid and the Ontario woodlands I'd loved and grown up in. I wasn't going to live with somebody who would abuse me no matter if they claimed to care for me like a lover or like family. I had to go. I was so shaken and scared by all this I decided I had to go far away, all the way out of the city.

So that's what I told my boss at the hospital. He not only gave me my last paycheque but my vacation pay. I know I've said you should work for all your luck, but it is also important to be like that boss: be generous when others need luck they can't make.

And this idiot boyfriend of mine, who had beat me so badly he broke my glasses, asked me for one last favour before I left him. He was so lazy he saw a last chance to make me do something for him, even though I had ended things with prejudice.

As I was packing my things to leave him behind, he said, "You have to go to the office anyway. Go and pick up my cheque, too, and deposit it." Like an idiot.

I didn't take all of his pay like I should have as recompense for the scare he'd put in me all the way to my bones. I took half of it, just what I needed to replace my glasses.

I was only fourteen when I first arrived in Toronto, you know. But then I left for good. And it was forty-four years before I went back.

I finally went back there for World Pride in 2014. I was maybe nineteen when I left Toronto for good and sixty-three or so when I returned. I was blown away by the buildings, how much the city had changed while I'd been gone.

When I had been there, it seemed like the shadow of the CN Tower could be seen anywhere in the city. I felt the shadow even heavier when I lived on the streets there. But when I went back in 2014, it felt like suddenly there were all these high-rises in the way.

Brick and stone stoops I'd slept in were gone, replaced with glass walls and bright LED lights and flashing ads and flashy mirrors.

It was so different from when I lived there, when I was young and impressionable. But I left while I was still young, still impressionable for all the jadedness that had been forced into me by then.

GROWING POTATO FROM SEED

I cashed out my whole cheque and all my savings after that boyfriend beat me.

I set out for Winnipeg again, where I'd make a home for about four years, not that I knew that when I arrived. I arrived by train the following evening after I'd left that boyfriend behind.

First thing I did was get a hotel room at the St. Charles Hotel. It was in a shady district, but it was just nice enough to get me a bed and a door with a working lock. I showered and found some food. Then I bought a newspaper to look for a job and saw an ad for kitchen help at the St. Boniface Hospital.

I was there in person first thing in the morning. I went in and said, "I used to work at Runnymede and would be perfect here. If you need a reference, I'll pay for the call."

It was a bluff, offering to pay for the call. Long distance calls were expensive for someone without even a permanent place to stay.

Luckily, they said, "We believe you," and hired me on the spot. Sometimes in life, you are lucky. I started in the dish room, washing. The fact that I was punctual and friendly enough to learn every language that wandered through my dish pit meant the menu clerk noticed me before she went on maternity leave.

She took me in as her replacement before she left. She used to bring me in on the weekend and train me. I wasn't paid to sit there and watch her collect and punch in the menu cards, but I knew it would get me a better job, even if just for a little while. Unpaid time was an investment in my future.

She showed me how to operate the machine that turned those handwritten menu cards into neat lists for the cooks. I call it a machine but it was a primitive computer whose only job was to manage who got what main course, who got cheese, who got nothing because their surgery was in the morning.

I met a lot of nice people there—a lot of Anishinaabe people as well. I used to go to the Mount Royal Hotel where all the gay and lesbian and trans folk hung out. My life was getting better there.

On my two weekends off, I got a job making microfiche of thirty years of invoices for some rich Jewish family. Ooh, their son was handsome. Whenever he used to glance over at me, I'd want to say, "Oh my god. You look *delicious*."

I also worked evenings at a bar on skid row. After a few years working there, I knew the regular bums from the regular patrons; I knew the good, decent people and we had become friends. Some I became very close with, especially this one lady of the night. We used to make sure to make each other laugh if we crossed paths; never a sombre moment between us.

One day, her brothers told me their mother had died and left them a house. It was a house suited to one person but all of them had families. They couldn't bear to sell the house or the memory or the investment the property could become.

They asked if I would move in, take over the utilities and keep the place from being vandalized. Of course I said yes. It was a small, safe home with a nice fenced backyard and straggly grass that was right next to a fire station.

One evening, as I left for work at the skid row bar, I overheard the firemen talking about spring planting, turning soil, gardening and growing your own food. I had grown up in Rocky Bay where my communities had been moved away from their gardens to rocky, ungrowable soil closer to settlers' roads.

In Rocky Bay, there were no gardens. It all sounded too romantic to me, pushing your hand into Mother Earth to sustain yourself. It seemed like the stories grandmothers in Rocky Bay had about what they used to grow and cultivate when we lived remotely on Lake Nipigon, near Grand Bay.

I told the firemen I wouldn't mind starting my own garden if only someone would turn the soil for such a delicate young woman like myself. To my surprise, when I got home, they had actually come around my fence and turned about half of my backyard into soft, mounded, rich soil. It was ready to be planted.

So on my next day off, I hurried happily to a garden centre. I went to the rack of seeds, picking out the best things for myself.

One of the things I wanted to grow was potato so I could make the fries I remembered eating at Dirty Gertie's little restaurant in Rocky Bay—eating the free food she would sneak us hungry kids who hung out on her deck dancing to the tunes she would play us on her jukebox.

After I'd been searching for a long time, clearly trying to add one more packet to the bunch I clutched, a garden centre clerk approached and asked what he could help me find. I told him I couldn't believe they didn't have potato seeds.

He laughed brightly before asking kindly, "Is this your first garden?"

"Why, yes," I said, wondering how he knew.

"Potato seeds are something you'll never find," he promised me. "You've probably already got what you need to grow potatoes if you have some at home."

"Well, I have potatoes from the store," I said.

I had no idea what he was implying. I'd never gardened before; how could I already have the makings of a potato seedling at home?

"Take one of those potatoes, cut it up and stick it in the dirt," he said. "It won't take long for the potato piece to sprout, and once the plant is nice and big, you can dig potatoes out of its roots. It's an easy plant!" he promised me.

So I bought the other seeds and went home to my potatoes. I cut it up the only way I knew how, like I'd been trained at any number of jobs. I washed the potato. I peeled it. I pressed it through my French fry cutter. I soaked them overnight like fries.

The next evening, I got dressed up all nice to look good for the firefighters who smoked on their breaks leaning on my fence where it met their alley. I made myself up like Eva Gabor on her

TV sitcom *Green Acres*. I might've been a touch more glamorous, with my long black hair coiffed for them to admire.

Looking good, I went to work with my pail of fries and stuck them into the ground. I'd make a hole with a stick and place in a fry. Move up the row of dirt, make a hole and place a fry. I did the same in other rows with my other seeds.

The firemen did watch me plant. They seemed more amused with my efforts than they were impressed with my lovely outfit. One of them called out, "This must be your first garden, eh?" I agreed, but man did I wonder how everybody knew that.

From then on, every second night before I left for work on skid row, I'd water my garden and flirt with the firemen. Things started growing, but no big potato plants like the man at the garden centre promised. I knew potatoes grew underground, so I figured it would be a matter of time before they ripened and pushed out a plant to tell me.

My peas grew nicely, but I waited and waited for my potatoes. I started to worry it would start to get too cold for them.

As the air started to turn to fall, I had a knock on my door. It was a pair of fireman, each with a sack of potatoes over their shoulder.

"You dug up my garden!" I said, flattered.

"No, ma'am," one told me. "You planted French fries. They were never gonna grow."

I couldn't believe it! I'd watered those rows of potatoes every other night for months!

"But thank you," the other said, giving me the two sacks I thought I'd been growing all along, "for the most entertaining summer we've ever had."

While living in Winnipeg, I learned so much about myself while watching others trying to be something they were not while I was just trying to be me.

I met people from all walks of life, every colour, poorest of the poor, people who were down and out and without a voice, people with no light at the end of the tunnel. These people became my circle of friends. These people had lived, laughed, had good jobs, and then something traumatic happened in their lives and they just sank down. Some started drugs and alcohol and couldn't recover. These people were never critical of my lifestyle, my feminine dress and the body so often perceived as masculine; they were so not judgmental.

Around that same time, I worked in a local restaurant, a German restaurant. I knew the owners' son from my work at the hotel where all the gay and lesbian and trans folk hung out. He got me the job but made me promise to never tell his parents he came down to the hotel.

So many of the workers there were illegitimate and some of the rooms belonged to sex workers. He wanted me to have the opportunity but didn't want his secrets spilled. So I sealed them away, no problem.

When they asked where we'd met, I said at the hospital where I worked. They were very kind so they told me to get to work, even assured me that I'd blend right in. Of course I didn't. I was deep-skinned and dark-haired and beautiful. All the other waitresses were blonde and blue-eyed and beautiful but fair.

But living in Winnipeg didn't last.

I loved how the airplane went out towards the ocean to make its landing into Vancouver. Going to Vancouver was a spur-of-the-moment trip for a long weekend which lasted for four months. You see, while I was in Vancouver, some purse snatchers got away with everything I had in my bag: my ID, money and plane tickets home. I was staying in an apartment hotel, but that didn't last long without any money or ID. So out on the street I went.

I had no choice. I had to hustle the streets, which wasn't easy in Vancouver. It was very territorial in those days and mostly controlled by pimps I wanted no part of. I managed to earn enough to get a new ID, and I used that to get on city welfare.

That got me a room in a cockroach-infested hotel on Hastings with enough for maybe one meal a day if I went to a cheap cafeteria in the area. I tried to eat only supper so I could sleep on a near-full stomach. Eventually I bumped into a working girl I knew from Winnipeg and we pooled our money to get a better room with a private bathroom and fewer pests. My welfare paid half and she covered the rest.

Vancouver was a party city then. There were foreign sailors and ships' crews and other people, mostly men, just passing through with money heavy in their pockets. I wasn't into the drinking or drugs that they spent so much on, but I did eat well when I entertained them. Needless to say, they expected favours in exchange for those full meals.

Vancouver was a nice place to visit but not to stay. It rained quite often. You can't tell because the city is built up so much with the concrete and steel buildings white people invented but the city is in a rainforest; it always wants to rain and there is nowhere for the water to go so you have to stomp through puddles on sidewalks and asphalt streets and alleys. You can never leave home without an umbrella.

I used to dance at the Smilin' Buddha Cabaret, and I loved Chinatown. I used to go to this restaurant that served nothing but dumpling and wonton soups. The most delicious soups. They were expensive, sometimes more than ten dollars, but they were so tasty I would splurge. That's ten dollars back then; I don't even care to figure out how much that would be now. But as an escort, I was always trying to save money, to build myself an emergency fund or a nest egg or whatever. I wanted to feel secure. Still, I couldn't always resist those delicious, decadent soups.

I wasn't in Vancouver long before I was run out of town. I was run out of town because I punched a police officer. I couldn't even pretend I didn't know he was an officer; he had his uniform on and everything.

He had cornered me and asked me for a blow job. I told him no, and he stepped closer and asked me again, so I told him to go to hell. He got rough and I punched him. He arrested me and drove me out of town, dropped me off on the side of the road.

I said, "To hell with you. Why would I give you a blow job? What do you think I am?"

He told me what he thought I was—a really colourful insult, so vivid and so mean—and I did not like it. I would've punched him again if I could've, it made me so mad. By then he was driving away. I've learned so much about being mean to other people by watching so many people trying to be something they were not. It's amazing. Like, get over your meanness and recognize that people are meant to be kind.

It made me so mad that I decided not to go back to Vancouver, so I hitchhiked to Calgary, through the mountains. I was very happy to hitch hike. I first walked a day and a half through the rise and fall of the mountainside highways. The mountains get cold, especially at night, and some of the highways are so steep on either side that there was nowhere to sleep but right in the gravel beside the road.

The driver who picked me up was looking for a chickie to get high with. He kept offering me drugs, kept insisting he had the good stuff. He couldn't understand someone who didn't want the good stuff. I tried to tell him that the only good stuff is the stuff that knocks you out for a doctor's surgery, but he wouldn't understand that.

Later, I figured he wanted to get me high so I'd owe him and he could get repayment in sex. Foolish. He should've seen how hungry I was and offered me a few all-I-could-eat meals. Maybe then I'd have obliged.

Once in Calgary, I went and had something to eat at White Spot. While I was there, I thought to myself, *Well, I would like to work in a place like this.* The servers were so friendly to each other, so open with the customers. It was brightly lit and very clean. I had been planning on just passing through, but I liked the restaurant. I liked the people. I liked the kind noise of the diners.

I went to the back office and knocked. There, I met a man called Mr. Steve Pappas. He founded White Spot (not that I realized I was barging in on the founder) and hired me on the spot. He didn't even have a job open, but he liked my ambition. He liked my smile.

He liked how open I was. I was able to talk about me, the truth, and he didn't have a problem. He even had another trans woman working for him, another Aboriginal woman at a different restaurant. Sometimes one open-minded man can change a lot of lives. Got me off the street. Kept her off the street. Gave us the dignity that only having a manager who will defend you can give, that a job that values your labour can give. It is not nothing to know that the real you, your chosen name and real self, are welcome at your place of work, amongst your coworkers, amongst the bosses.

But he didn't hire me to be revolutionary or even progressive. He hired me for my pretty smile. If I tried to get a job on only my smile at this age, they'd tell me I was crazy! I've been told I was crazy many times. Maybe I am. Maybe I'm not.

This is crazy: I once had an office job.

I worked with this guy and noticed he fell behind on his paperwork. He had things written down here and there but nothing was in order and nothing was filed. I told him, "You gotta let me help you get this sorted or you're going to get fired. It has to get filed."

So for an entire week, after I rushed through all of my work, I would come and help him sort and file things and organize his desk. After a whole week of helping him, he insisted he take me out to dinner to thank me, and he insisted we go anywhere I wanted. So I chose a new Portuguese restaurant nearby; I'd heard they had good fish.

We got there, and it was indeed a beautiful restaurant and the service was smooth and unhurried. When it came time to order, I ordered a dozen smelts.

The waiter lost his smooth countenance and boggled at me.

"You want a dozen smelts?"

Smelts are little fish, about six inches long. They're so small you can eat them whole. I assured him I could eat three dozen if I wanted; I often did as a child in one sitting.

When the waiter came with our food, it was with a giant platter. Heads turned. Other patrons stared. The waiter placed the largest smelts I had ever seen in front of me. They were as big as a proper fish; they were a foot long and huge and there was a dozen of them. I literally asked the waiter what the hell he'd brought me.

"Smelts," he said.

So I ate as much as I could and we took the rest back to our homes. My colleague insisted on paying despite my mistake. But at our next staff meeting, he warned everyone not to invite me to dinner or they'd have to max out their Visa.

He wasn't making fun of me. We had bonded. It was what community was supposed to mean: enjoying each other's foibles, providing for each other, doing each other's paperwork and eating each other's extra fish.

Coming from a reserve, you don't know everything about the outside world. One of my first times out to a steak dinner, the person I was with said, "I'll have a steak, medium." I didn't know any different, so I said, "I'll have a steak, too, large."

A SHELTER OR A HOME

I briefly lived in Quebec City. It was one of the priciest cities in Canada. It was a historic city, a tourist city. The locals moved slowly and the tourists hurried through, always bringing new money.

It had everything a city had to offer, but it moved at a much slower pace. I had a very small apartment on Rue Hamel, just behind the Hôtel-Dieu, the "Hostel of God," situated right in the fortress of Fort Saint-Jean. I spent six months there. I got a job as a server in one of the many cafés; English speakers were desirable workers anywhere where American tourists were spending money.

I went running each morning. Started by running up the stairs near Theatre Frontenac, through the Plains of Abraham and back to the entrance of the fort itself. I lived there in spring and summer. In summer, Quebec City is full of life and rich with entertainment. I marvelled at the music that seemed to bloom throughout the city and its parks. I went to a park each evening I wasn't working at the café. Each evening presented a different artist, singer or dance show. I saw everything from comedy to jazz.

The best part: It was all free. It made the city feel like a fantasy, that high art was available for the public. It was pure peacetime. The heat of the summer was invigorating, not suffocating, with cool evenings and mornings and bright afternoons.

But one day there was a riot at the St. Jean Baptiste celebrations. Thousands of rioters in nationalist flags descended on the parks. Then hundreds of cops with riot gear and billy clubs and shields and water canons followed. All of us who wanted to revel in the free art and entertainment were sent home; many of us fled home without being told.

People were freaking out; the peaceful people of Quebec City had never seen such violence at their lovely parks during free concerts. It spread out of the park and into the city. The men with flags smashed windows and looted and pushed people down onto the glassy sidewalks.

For me though, it was like being back on the rez when neighbours fought. In our territory, before the white man relocated us, one had to paddle a few miles to start a fight, so you calmed down by the time you arrived. You talked it out because you knew you needed the energy in your arms to paddle back.

On the rez, with all the prefab houses on little lots, fights broke out all the time amongst those not used to living in each other's pockets and on each other's nerves. It was only the cops and the water cannons that were new to me. But I kept calm as I fled the cops.

After that, there were more cops on the streets. And my quiet runs in the mornings and the peaceful park concerts were no more. It had been Quebec nationalists who started the riots, but the police spotted me as an outsider. I started getting harassed every day by transphobic, racist cops. I'd walk through the beautiful architecture of the city and be constantly stopped and frisked. It ruined my love of the city.

It wasn't the priciness that made me leave; it was how unwelcome I became.

The cops were on high alert and the beauty of the city only made their harshness seem harder. So I moved on.

I moved to Montreal. Montreal seemed as friendly as Quebec City had been, but it had some of the hustle and bustle that stopped people from noticing anyone but themselves. I could walk without harm again.

I used to dance flamenco in a Spanish restaurant in Montreal. They had a Spanish guitarist. And I went there on a date, actually. I liked the music, and I asked the waiter, "Do you mind if I get up and dance?"

"Go ahead," he said.

So I started to dance.

"Where did you learn that?" he asked me when I was done.

I learned from the Roma in Paris, France.

I couldn't live in France. The Roma man whom I dated when I was there, he wanted me to stay. But I couldn't stay. I only had one love after Eric, only developed trust in one other person like that. It didn't last and I couldn't seek it out again. I felt stronger on my own, carrying memories of love rather than seeking the actions of some new romance.

I carried the memories of love everywhere. Once, while living in Montreal, I grew brave enough to watch fireworks for the first time since Eric died. It was some kind of competition, with the fireworks synced to music, so the lights and sound danced together.

I was sharing a bench with people I didn't know, but I found words breaking out of me with my tears.

"I'm crying my eyes out," I couldn't help but say.

"Me too!" said a woman beside me. "Oh, it's so beautiful!"

And it was beautiful. But it wasn't beauty that was making me cry. It was so beautiful, but at the same time it brought me back to that night on Centre Island. It brought me back to that last night with Eric. It brought to the surface of my heart how much I missed him.

I dated a lot of different guys, a lot of professional men. I used to go to concerts and other events with them, all dressed up like I was their escort. I used to joke that I should do this professionally. Because I learned from working with escorts and prostitutes that a lot of men are not looking for sex. They're looking for company, looking for conversation. They're looking to vent. They're looking to believe they've been understood.

Understanding is important; if we are not understood, we are not known, as people. To be loved, to be seen, someone has to know us.

Sometimes, even the people closest to us don't understand us.

They say there's one black sheep in every family. I was a herd of black sheep.

I have come to the conclusion, in my adulthood, that as dysfunctional as I may be, my whole family's dysfunctional. What I fought against all my life exists in my own family: drug abusers, womanizers, woman beaters, rapists, drunks. My sister Molly once told me, "Oh, you're not cool. You don't smoke dope." I guess I'm not cool.

It's always just been easier to be sober.

I did try dope—cannabis—once. It was the night before a friend's wedding. The bride gathered us bridesmaids and we smoked; it was my first time. I didn't know what it meant to be high, I felt just overwhelmingly hungry. I couldn't stop the hunger. I ate two and a half loaves of bread and an entire jar of peanut butter. There was nothing I could do to restrain myself. Being high was just being hungry and irrational. I couldn't get the toaster to toast fast enough.

The morning came, my high had faded. Unfortunately, I had eaten so much bread and I had bloated so much that we couldn't get my dress on. I had to rush out and buy one of those waist cinchers to pull in my bread-laden gut enough to zip my zipper.

It's just easier to be sober. I wouldn't have eaten two and a half loaves on my own, after all. Being high, being drunk … it can lead to its own form of trouble.

The first time I got drunk was on my fortieth birthday. I was living in Montreal then, and I just took myself out for a special night. I remember ordering a gin and tonic, sipping on it and gagging, then sipping again and gagging. The second drink tasted a little better.

But that's all I remember—trying the second drink.

After that, suddenly, in a flash that took an eternity, I woke up uncomfortable. I was so cold; the bed was hard and scratchy. This was back in the days when all the girls were trying to look like Twiggy, so my first thought was that I'd eaten crackers in lieu of dinner in my bed the night before and that crackers in my sheets were why I was so scratchy.

I cracked open my eyes. I saw a set of tires. I rolled over. Another set of tires.

I was cold because I was naked. I was uncomfortable because someone had left me between two parked cars, naked, discarded, in the near-freezing cold. Someone had left me there, had taken my clothes but left me with my purse. I had to try to stop a car or flag a taxi. People kept driving by; I must have looked crazy with my long hair and no clothes, all scraped up from sleeping in a parking lot.

Finally, a taxi pulled over.

"You have to phone in," the driver told me. "We don't just pick people up."

Oh, how crazy I must've looked.

"I'm just trying to get home," I said. "I don't know what's happened."

"Where's your clothes?" he asked me.

"I don't know," I admitted. "I just want to go home."

I think he took pity on me.

"Do you have money?" he asked.

I had a few dollars in my purse. He gave me a blanket from the back of his taxi, let me climb in. He started driving and I tried to give him directions, but I quickly realized I didn't know what streets we were driving.

The taxi driver had no idea what street I was asking about. He'd never heard my address before. Finally he realized how lost I was.

"This is Winnipeg," he told me.

I could feel shock bloom in my expression. I saw sympathy mirror in his face as he no doubt imagined women in his life as lost and naked as I was. Vulnerable.

I'd started my night in Montreal. Now I was naked and alone in Winnipeg with no memories of who took me there, how or why. The taxi driver took me to the police station.

I filled out the report on what happened to me, but I didn't have a single useful detail. The cops phoned some of their wives, who brought me some clothes.

That was on July 4. My birthday is on June 29. I have no recollection of the time between my birthday and waking up.

I suppose I'd been drugged. I don't have a lot of experience being drunk, but I don't think most drunks lose four days each time they fall off the wagon. I didn't drink after that for years. It's only recently that I've imbibed again and only with my friends who go to the theatre with me. We'll share a chocolate martini after a show.

I told my cousin the story of my birthday when I was drugged once I had gotten safely back to Montreal. She was aghast, shocked.

"Oh, you could've woken up dead!" she told me, as if that was a reasonable warning.

I laughed. If I'd ended up dead, I simply wouldn't have woken up.

When I was living in Montreal, I ran short of money. I had a place to stay but I was chronically short of money. It had been many, many years since I was homeless in Toronto but still, sometimes, the money would run out.

I went to a grocery store one night after I got off work and asked if I could work for a couple of hours stocking shelves in exchange for a sandwich from the deli.

They said no.

But I was so hungry.

The aisles were brightly lit and sparklingly clean but for the slush of Montreal underfoot. The shelves were stocked with vibrantly-coloured boxes and shiny glass jars and tempting fruits. The store was filled to the brim with food and opportunity and yet I was being told no, none for you.

I was so hungry that I stole two slices of meat and a dry bun. I got caught shoplifting.

They even called the police, who arrested me over the dry bun and two slices of ham. I was so hungry, but I got caught before I even got to eat.

Because I had touched the food, they threw it away.

So I got arrested. Sat in the backseat of a car in handcuffs like a criminal. Spent a night in jail. I was still so hungry. They'd thrown my pitiful sandwich away.

When I went to court, I got lucky.

The judge thought that overseeing a shoplifting case because of a dry bun and two slices was a waste of the court's time. He saw that I was struggling, but working, and that I had asked to work for it before I took what I needed to survive. In a way, the people who called the cops were the thieves. They stole the time of the cops, the jailers, the judge; that all cost more than any sandwich I could've stolen.

The judge told me he would let me off completely if I would agree to two conditions. First, I had to promise not to steal again and look harder for charity next time. Second, to repay the judge's charity, I'd have to do community service.

He said, "But don't do it again. I'm not gonna book anyone over something like this. But you go find someplace to take you for community work."

So I started looking for community programmes and centres and other places. Nobody would take me. I was Anishnaabe, and French was my third or fourth language so my accent was so strange no one knew where this Anishnaabe person could be from. I was like an alien even though I looked and dressed as the normal woman I was.

Luckily, I found Chez-Doris.

Chez-Doris was a daytime drop-in centre.

It was named after Doris, an Aboriginal woman who worked as a prostitute. In the cold of Montreal, when she was alive, she used to yearn for a place where she could go and sit and no one would judge her for her job, where no one would shoo her away for loitering, where she wouldn't have to disclose her job or her problems to be welcome, where she didn't need to be sick or dying or feel pathetic to deserve help.

Doris wanted a safe place to sit and play cards with her friends.

Ladies in Upper Westmont got together in Montreal and started Chez-Doris in a basement. They created that safe, social space dedicated to support and community. By the time they got it running, Doris had been dead for a few years. She'd been murdered and her body left in the road like carrion. It's still unsolved.

Chez-Doris was a space that could put me back on a good path, could provide the support I needed to start finding good luck again. So when the judge sentenced me to community service, that's where I went.

Did you know the Humane Society existed before any children's aid in Canada? And we had homeless shelters for men but not women. Women were so associated with labour in the home that there wasn't room for them on the street. They didn't even have the squalor of homelessness to escape to if they were dealing with abuse; no one would make room for a beaten woman. No room in any inn or stable, not for women like us.

Chez-Doris was one of the only places that made room.

I started off in the basement. On the first day after the manager agreed to give me a place to work, I came down the stairs to that basement and had a profound thought:

I thought, *Holy shit. I'm a fool for wearing these heels; I'm liable to bust my head.* It was such a low basement that I spent my first day ducking and every other day in flat shoes.

Eventually, my charity was paid back in the eyes of the judge. My time was up. And to my delight, Chez-Doris hired me. So I finished my punishment for stealing and Chez-Doris gave me this good path to walk. Sometimes, you can be very lucky, but luck usually follows a bit of hard work. The good path in Anishinaabemowin is called "minodahmun." And I'd found it.

I loved my job and they clearly thought I had the skills, but I felt like an imposter. I knew I had never done any real training for my job. Sure, I spoke a lot of languages, but I had never gotten any real education. I'd never even believed I was smart enough for an education. If you think you're too dumb for a certificate or a diploma, it's hard to believe you deserve to do the kind of work those bits of paper usually gatekeep people from.

One day, I was walking by this old building on Sherbrooke Street to the ghetto near McGill University where I lived. I walked by it dozens of times before I went in. I was looking around and this man came up to me and said, "Can I help you?"

I said, "What is this place?"

"It's an annex of a private college out in the east end," he told me. "Are you thinking of starting classes?"

I hadn't been thinking of classes at all. I couldn't help but blurt, "I didn't even finish eighth grade. I thought I was too old to go to college anyway."

I was decades past when I should have finished high school, and I really believed I was too old to learn anything from a job site anymore.

"No," he told me. "Most of the students here are adults."

It sparked something in me. I would love to learn. I always had loved learning, but I couldn't stay in school after I left home. Suddenly, what I thought I had given up was possible again. It was like I had gone back in time and my future was in front of me, anew. I decided, yes, I was thinking of starting classes.

The man sent me in to talk to the dean of admissions. She listened to my story, and she said, "I think you've got a lot of smarts. How about this? We'll give you your first two courses for free."

I signed up for Introduction to Psychology and a course about bringing proper nutrition to daycares. I would sit in the lectures and listen so hard I'd get a headache. I'd read and read until the lines blurred together. I felt like I had to work hard to make up for all the school I had missed, but I could also relate to the ideas of the teachers and my peers. I could follow along, I could analyze. I knew how to draw inferences that weren't obvious to everyone.

When the semester ended, I got my marks.

I made a 97 and a 98.

I couldn't believe it. What was even more difficult to believe was that, because I did so well, I earned a scholarship. I even earned a residency allowance. I already had a place to live, so I sublet the scholarship housing to someone else. I felt more secure than I had in a long time. I was working harder than I ever had, but I had a home—technically I even had a tenant—and it was all because I had made good choices and kept working hard.

And then I did believe it. I believed my good grades. I believed I deserved my scholarship. I believed all the potential my bosses at Chez-Doris saw. To believe it, I had to realize I wasn't stupid. All my life my mother told me I wasn't gonna amount to anything, that I was stupid. She had had me believing that.

But holy shit, I had kept up in those classes, and more than that I had actually done really well. It was like a hunger was woken up within me. I registered for four more courses and kept my full-time job.

When I went back to school full-time, there were about 240 of us in different disciplines, and we were all women of colour—Chinese, Filipino, Black, Asian, African. The best ideas come from mixed groups. Every good mix will have at least one savage.

Once, during one of our intensive art classes, I heard two of the white students saying to each other that the students of colour were getting more credit than their art deserved. They kept saying things like, "Oh, those kind of people are naturally good at art; it's not real skill." Those kind of people this, those kind of people that.

They couldn't stand that the students of colour were being praised when they weren't. They had to invent this whole idea that we were naturally better, like the pigment in our skin helped us draw, that it wasn't simply that we had happened to make more time to practice. I one class on a Sunday in the afternoon, we had to close up and clear up the classroom. The teacher asked me if I'd hang back to help clean brushes.

"You know what?" I said, pointing to the white kids who said those things. "I really think those kinds of people might do a better job cleaning."

One time those same people asked me how I knew so much about art. I didn't have that silver-spoon background they expected of people who knew art theory.

That's the thing about theory: You can study and think and study and think, and then when you meet someone who's spent all that time practicing, you're suddenly outpaced. Experience is the best. I had no background of going to museums or taking art classes in high school—I didn't even finish high school—but I'd always practiced art, even when the only practice was the fantasies I lived in.

I used to live in fantasy. Sometimes when I was terribly hungry as a child, I would go into this meditative state almost like hibernation. It would dull the pain and I would stare at the food magazines and imagine a dinner for myself so vividly I could taste it.

Overall, I loved that class. I learned so much. There was so much culture. We learned so much from each other because each person, each tribe of people, handled things a different way and came to the same solution. It showed how many different ways of thinking there are.

There was even a student who stood up and gave an excellent oral report, wonderful. She barely looked down at her notes. I was so impressed. I learned that the teacher said he didn't know how to mark it.

"It was a good presentation," he said. "But she didn't write anything down. It's just chicken scratch she was reading from, and she turned nothing in."

After investigating, it turned out the young woman was so well spoken she'd literally talked her way into school. She had hoped to keep her illiteracy hidden until it wasn't a problem anymore, until she'd learned enough to be literate. She stayed hungry to learn, even when people said they couldn't even measure if she had progressed.

I stayed in school long enough to graduate, but I missed my college graduation because I was in Greece. I figured I had worked so hard for so long to get that diploma and I had a choice of celebrating that hard work by hiding under a gown and cap or by basking under an umbrella.

So I went to Greece. It was so hot that all I could do all day was bask, like a captive, happy turtle under a sun lamp. At night when it was cool, it was time to go out and dance. And eventually it was time to return to Turtle Island, to Canada, to work.

Eventually, my boss at Chez-Doris got hungry for more too. She took me with her when she began bigger projects.

We opened up the first mental health crisis centre in Canada. It was an enormous undertaking; sometimes, looking back, I can't believe we pulled it off. We had to find a space, we had to figure out if we were commercial or non-profit, we had to get every pen and desk chair and paper clip triple-quote, budget-approved, we had to find insurance for a crisis centre, a thing that had never been insured before. On top of that, we had to market ourselves and actually become a crisis centre, a resource people knew or recognized.

Oh, it was a damn big job. I could open anything now that I know I went through this.

It was an incredible amount of work. But I'd do it again in a heartbeat. If I came across the money for it, I'd open a day centre for women here in Thunder Bay. And I mean for women—not for kids, not for mothers' resources. Those spaces are important, of course, but it's also important to have child-free spaces. Mothers need to come in and decompress and have time to process the things they can't talk about in front of their kids. Or maybe they've lost their kids, to drugs or to the system, and seeing kids at the centre would make them stop coming or would be too much.

But it's hard to come across money for women and women only. For suffering women, especially.

Once I had that job, that education, it seemed like people treated me a little better. White people especially would treat me better. By better, I mean they treated me like a person for once. It was like they saw I was working hard and was capable and they were able to temporarily set their biases aside.

Some people would leave their biases aside, but some would pick their prejudice right back up. I suppose if they saw past all their biases they'd have to make room for more compassion and kindness. Those take more work to carry.

It would also require them to create an image of themselves that was not reliant on believing they were better than those they were biased against. Without an image of those they were better than, what made them valuable? If they weren't better than brown people, how did they know they were anything at all?

After a while, Chez-Doris took over a famous old building in Montreal called the Quaker Building, just a few buildings away from the Montreal Forum.

It used to be a merchant's fancy house before the Quakers bought it in the sixties and turned it into their meeting house. It used to house their day school and their meetings and was the operations centre for all their charity. The house had even sheltered draft dodgers from the Vietnam War. Quaker women made the pilgrimage from the house to the US border and returned with back seats stuffed with young pacifist men.

The lovely century-old home served as the Quaker meeting house for decades before its constant need for upkeep and renovations began to outpace their budget. They reluctantly sold the building, but I imagine it was a solace to sell something they didn't want to lose to a shelter like Chez-Doris. We bought the building for one dollar.

It was a beautiful place, decorated in the sixties and seventies by the McGill University architect Jonas Lehrman. The home was so lovely that the ladies Chez-Doris served stopped coming.

The beautiful house was too visible, too exposed to be a drop-in centre. It had too much cold, expensive marble to be a warm home for the centre. So I did some scouting. We found an old mansion nearby, down a side street, and we convinced the owner to exchange buildings with us. He got that beautiful building on the main road, just inches from the Forum, and we had a place that was just as pretty but hidden enough for the ladies to drop-in again.

Before we left that spot next to the Forum, the location attracted an incredible visitor: Tina Turner herself came to see us.

She was so real, so vibrant, so lifelike. She glowed with life and looked you right in the eye and could see who you were. She could see what you carried. She visited and stayed with us for a day, speaking to the women, to the workers like me. She donated $3000, which would be worth nearly seven grand today.

We also had a famous visitor before he was famous. When he was a boy, Patrick Roy's mother Maria would volunteer at the centre. Her husband would bring their boys and they would dig up our garden, planting things, teaching anyone who asked how to make space more beautiful. They were a kind family, and they spent time at Chez-Doris making it look and feel more like a home.

Eventually an old lady from Upper Westmont—where the really rich people lived—died and we found out she left Chez-Doris nearly four million dollars. We took the 3.7 million and we renovated the entire building.

We put in an excellent, beautiful commercial kitchen; that kitchen was so nice I still dream about it all these years later.

Eventually, that money ran out and Chez-Doris began to struggle again. I was long gone, but the same problems the Quaker House had were creeping up: old buildings needed new repairs and that took real money. In 2018, someone else left a million dollars to Chez-Doris. They took that money and not only did their repairs but expanded. They own the house across the street now, too, and even run a shelter with nearly thirty apartments. They help women like Doris out of homelessness before they become another unsolved murder, a wasted OD, or worse.

I had good luck finding Chez-Doris; it put me on a good path and the work I did there taught me I had smarts and empathy and value and values.

But soon it was time to go home. I'd been moving around since I was about fourteen, and it had been decades since I'd had a sense of what home was. It had been decades since I left Rocky Bay. The idea of it as home felt more like the idea of a mythical past by then. I'd spent so many years in other places and far more time away than I had growing up there.

It feels silly now, at the elderly age I am now, but in Montreal, I started to feel old. I was only in my forties or so (at a certain age, a lady stops telling), but I was feeling old.

I was ready to go home. For it had been so, so long since I'd had a real one.

But I knew where my family was. Many of them had left Rocky Bay too. They went to Thunder Bay for jobs or to be closer to doctors or just to be closer to each other. So when it was time for me to answer the call of my heart to find a home again, I went back to Thunder Bay.

WHAT TAKES OR GIVES A LIFE

Being in Thunder Bay led me closer to my family, geographically, if not emotionally. Some of my siblings, even after decades of me living as a woman, didn't accept it. Stuck in colonial bigotry, they forgot or couldn't accept that trans people would have been loved by our ancestors. So they held me at a distance.

Being in Thunder Bay also meant that when I got sick, I was close to where I needed to be anyway. When people need dialysis here in the north, they often have to go to Kenora or Thunder Bay to be close enough to the machines that can keep them alive. But I'd already made Thunder Bay my home.

Dialysis has defined a lot of the last years of my life. I spend so much time in the dialysis unit that I've carved out a home there, with nurse friends and patient friends and doctor friends, and with a job as a patient-family advisor. I sell baked goods and meat pies at the hospital to whoever wants some.

Once, a nurse ordered four dozen butter tarts on Wednesday. I took them to her on a Thursday. At the end of the day, she came to me just shaking, vibrating. She said, "Can you make me one more order? I tried one and they were so good I kept eating. I think I ate them all. Four dozen." I couldn't believe it! She joked she was so full of butter and sugar but it was the embarrassment that would kill her.

Some of the nurses asked me once, "Can you give us your recipe for your pie crust?"

I said, "No, it's my pie crust. If you want crust, you buy it from me."

Recipes, after all, are the only happy secrets.

When I first got sick with kidney disease, I had the symptoms of a depressed person. I was withdrawn and not interested in anything. Every thought exhausted me; it was like my brain was filled with gel and the impulses of my neurons couldn't get through. I was tired down to my bones, and I couldn't understand why I was gaining weight. I'm not a big eater, so when I became depressed and exhausted, I ate even less. But I was getting bigger and bigger.

I didn't understand it, but I was so fatigued and apathetic that nothing mattered, not even my body doing things that made no sense. It was slowly filling with heaviness and weighing me down. I lost energy. Hauling in air, I was too tired to notice it was harder than it should be just to breathe.

Finally one day, I was walking to my car and I just couldn't breathe. I was so heavy. I had gotten so fat, it seemed. I know now it was all the water my kidneys couldn't take out of me; I was just waterlogged with every toxin your body usually filters. I knew I had to get to the hospital, but I couldn't drive in that condition.

When the first bus arrived, I didn't have enough energy to lift my leg enough to make the big step onto the bus. The driver said I should wait for the next bus because it could lower for people like me who couldn't make the big step.

I waited for about fifteen minutes and then rode the bus to the hospital. The walk from the bus stop to that hospital seemed longer than I'd ever walked in my life. I couldn't breathe, but I made it just inside the doorway before I passed out. I'd had a total arrest.

It was lucky I had made it to the doors, that I hadn't collapsed somewhere someone would have to come across me. I don't know if I would have had that time; I was being suffocated in my own body.

They saved me, got me breathing, got me heavily medicated. That's when I started dialysis.

Most people go through this thing on dialysis: You go through the stages of dying.

You realize your own mortality because without a machine propping you up, you'd die. You realize your own mortality because you see someone skip one session and never recover; you realize your own life is just as precarious.

You die in one small way or another when you have that kind of dependency. You can't travel the same way because you need to be in the same chair a few times a week to stay healthy. You can't eat and drink anything you want because the machine can only do so much to remove toxins from your blood. Your life changes, and in some ways it gets smaller, more routine.

But dialysis gives you more time. It gives you your life back.

You know, sometimes I thought my life was just a bad dream. And I couldn't wake up or get out of it.

I spent a lot of time in the church; it was my refuge. Contrary to what they say about the Catholic Church, I always felt safe there. I still go to church often, and I still feel very safe there. I wasn't Christian, I just wanted to get away. The church offers such good solitude, such peaceful feelings and a chance not to hear aggressive words.

Once, I had an Anishnaabe nurse ask me what I did on my days off, the days I don't come in for dialysis. I told her that I often went to church.

"Are you that religious?" she asked me, sounding surprised.

I suppose too many religious people are so committed to their dogmas they forget the point is to be kind to those around you. So she was surprised that I attended church but wasn't judgmental or cruel like the church leaders that ran residential and day schools were.

"No, no," I explained. "I find solitude in the church. When I was a child, it was the only place I found refuge."

I spent a lot of time in church as a child. I would dust the pews. I would straighten the hymnals. The Father was a very, very decent man. I talked to talk to him about my problems, but he really couldn't do anything.

We lived so remotely and in such a small community, any report would make its way to my mother before it made its way to Children's Aid. We thought that report would make my mother so angry she'd kill me.

Besides, what were the chances anything would get better for me if I were taken away? Maybe I'd be abused somewhere else and not have my siblings or anyone else I loved around to have good times with too. I trusted the Father a lot. I told him everything.

I explained to the nurse, "At church, nobody abused me. Nobody talked bad to me. It was always very nice there."

When I explain why I found comfort in religion, people aren't usually as surprised. For some it's the community; for some it's the expectation that they'll study and apply morality to their life; for some it's just about the peace and quiet and the order always present in the space. When someone learns you find comfort in a tradition like church, the why of it is usually all they need to understand.

Instead, this nurse pressed on. She demanded to know if I'd ever been abused by the priests in the Catholic Church. I told her, truthfully, no. She then said to me, "Well, then I guess it pays to be ugly."

I was so shocked. I wish I had said, "Holy shit, have you looked in the mirror, lady?" But I was so surprised I said nothing more.

Usually, my experience with nurses in dialysis in Thunder Bay is much better. There are exceptions. For example, some of the nurses were laid off during the pandemic because they refused to get the COVID-19 vaccine when it became available. They refused with such commitment that they would rather lose their jobs.

It made no sense to me. To be a nurse, you must promote health. You take classes, you learn science. You work with medicines and sick people every day and then refuse to protect us? Refuse to protect yourself? It was so strange to me, stranger than that woman's surprise that I was a churchgoer.

Some of the young nurses who replaced them didn't know enough yet. It compromised our care. They didn't maintain the sterile field when they were getting the dialysis access set up. It scared me. I fought so hard to stay healthy, and the idea that a young nurse could sabotage me with a simple, preventable infection scared me so.

Still. I'm happy here, on dialysis.

Thunder Bay, nowadays, it's one of the best places I've lived.

Still, it is strange to live your life on dialysis.

My cousin Gertie died on dialysis.

One of her sons and a daughter died on dialysis. And her sister died and the other four daughters died of diabetes. One by one, a tiny molecule called sugar ripped them apart from the inside, killing their nerves and their kidneys and destroying their future.

Diabetes is one of those diseases that I wish people took more seriously. All it takes to fight it is to maintain a proper diet and to exercise. But people get funny when they lose the autonomy of good health; they won't follow a routine or listen to doctors. They let their sugars get out of control and they lose time they should have had if they stayed healthy.

The same thing happens with dialysis patients. They're told to avoid certain foods and just can't do it. So much of the control they had over their life has been lost to their failing kidneys, yet they try to regain control by bucking instructions.

Sometimes I wonder if there's some kind of reverse psychology we could use to make people listen. You know, like if they told these people dialysis they can eat whatever they like from a list instead of telling them what to avoid. Just give them a list of instructions and they'll probably follow the diet.

It seems like once you tell them something to avoid, it moves into their head rent free. They end up craving it all the time and they have to have it.

I do dialysis a few times a week. It takes a lot of time, and it takes a lot out of you. You're bound to this machine and this chair, and it is more exhausting than you can imagine to have your blood pulled out of you and cleaned. I would have never thought hours of sitting would leave me wiped and tired, but it does. But it also keeps me from filling with fluid and toxins, too weak to lift my leg to get on the bus.

Recently, someone in the dialysis unit was upset. He was angry about how many days and how many hours a week he had to sit in the dialysis chair.

"Dialysis is taking up my whole fucking life!" he said.

I told him, "That's where you're wrong. Dialysis is giving you your life." Being the nosy person I am, I went on to ask him, "What do you do after dialysis each day?"

"Well, nothing," he admitted.

"And what do you do before dialysis each day?" I asked.

"Nothing," he said.

So I went on, "What do you do on your days off, between dialysis?"

He said nothing.

And I even went further and I asked, "What kind of job did you do before you had to have dialysis?"

He sort of shrugged. "I've never worked."

And I said, "You're thirty-five, thirty-six and you've never worked? What is it you were doing with your life before dialysis? Seems like you're doing just as much now."

He got so angry with me. "You don't understand!" he shouted. "You don't know what it's like to be an Aboriginal and try to look for a job!"

It was preposterous. It took all my effort not to punch him. What did he think I am? I'm clearly not white. I'm clearly not Black. I'm clearly not Asian. It is clear that I, too, know what it was like to look for work as an Aboriginal. He was just so caught up in maintaining his position as a victim, maintaining what faults weren't his, that he didn't see me in front of him at all.

I will be fair: It can be harder to get a job now than it was. I got all kinds of odd jobs when I was homeless, like dishwashing for a hotel or a club.

Nowadays, to get that same job, the requirements include a tenth-grade education. I didn't have that. Some dishwashing jobs even require you to have a SmartServe certification, something else I didn't have, and I don't understand how you'd have the time to get if you were hungry on the streets like I used to be. I would have had a harder time getting the same jobs today than I did as a homeless kid then.

But I still would not have given up. I would have endured and tried and persevered. I would have made it. I did make it.

But it would have been harder to pull myself up by my bootstraps if they'd been covered in red tape.

People forget that sometimes it takes just one reason to end up on the street. I knew a homeless man who had had a good job as an engineer. One day, while he was at work, his wife and three kids died in a fire. And he just lost everything. He lost his mind. He lost his family, lost his home and lost his sobriety, which cost him his job. He lost himself. That's the sad part. He lost himself. He actually made me cry when I met him. I didn't know how he could begin to put himself back together.

Another time, as I was leaving the hospital, I saw an East Indian woman. She didn't look happy. I went up to her and offered her a hug. She burst out crying and accepted. I held her while she cried. She thanked me profusely when we separated, but I did nothing special. I just knew she needed a hug. I saw her as a whole person, and I knew what she needed.

It isn't hard to see people as whole, complicated people, but sometimes even smart people forget. For a long time, a doctor might see you as your problem, not as their patient. They'd see a failing kidney and they wouldn't treat the person but the kidney. They have rounds at the hospital now that are multidisciplinary. It's about time.

Since I began dialysis in Thunder Bay, I've thought the rounds they did before, single-disciplinary rounds, were wrong. The most important person there ought to have been the patient. But instead a doctor would go around to each of the patients in his clinic, talk to each of them and ask them questions. Sometimes a medical student would trail him, and teaching the student was more important than checking on the patient. And then you would never hear from the doctor again.

Some orders would be written in a chart and you, the patient, would be left alone. Some other doctor would come through and read hasty notes about you, and you'd never see them at all.

I always thought that the job wasn't being done right. Finally, for the first time, the patient is able to give their input on their own case. Because the most important person ought to be the patient: the person the doctor is talking about.

Before, the doctors might get this information about their patients every six months. Now it's information they know all the time. They actually keep track of what each person is going through now; they're more than just the numbers in their bloodwork. They're people again.

Knowing the actual patient is an important part of the practice. There are lots of unconscious ways we look out for our community members, after all, that we wouldn't even notice we exclude strangers from. It's good to know your patient as a person, to know what their other doctors are doing about their care, to get together with all their professionals and agree on how the patient is doing.

My friend Bea used to be a renal nurse before she got sick. She seemed to get sick so suddenly and then the doctors told her she had two weeks left. That was five years ago. She put up a good long fight. She and I were theatre friends. We used to go to the theatre together, and sometimes we would go for a drink and chat afterwards.

Her son almost always accompanied us as our chauffeur and he would always complain about it. Once, I pulled him aside and reminded him that just because she ignored all natural logic when she survived the two weeks she'd been given didn't mean she wasn't still dying. She was his dying mother who was well enough to live a life that she shared with him at the theatre. I told him how he would miss it when she was gone. How he would regret complaining.

I wonder if she missed working in the renal unit in those last years. When she got sick, she had to stop working. When I got sick, I stopped working, too, but ended up in the renal unit. She got sick and had to leave.

I loved working. I had so many jobs, even once worked as a special education worker. I loved it. I loved working with kids. I'm lucky enough to be well enough that I work part-time now and I often have the pleasure of working with kids.

Working special ed when I was younger, I had to break down tasks for the child into smaller tasks. A lot of the time the child would be stuck not because of the task itself but because of difficulty in just one area. If I broke it down step by step by step, we found where the difficulty was and we worked on that till the difficulty was overwritten.

I also like sitting on committees at the hospital. They ask, "What are we doing right?" And I get to say, "Nothing."

That's what I like about it. And I'm a voice not only for the patients but for the nurses. The nurses can say what they want to me. They can complain to me and I get to complain louder. Because the nurse who complains professionally has to complain to someone above her, who has power over her, who can silence her with a threat or a firing. But I'm a patient on the committee. They can't fire me.

After all, dialysis is what gave me back my life. It's too big to fire me from.

Once I was walking along at night, around ten o'clock. A man came up to me and asked if I wanted to buy some dishes. He showed me what he had—they were obviously stolen; brand-new in a telltale way—so I said no.

A little while later, another man came up to me and asked if I was selling drugs. I told him no. A little while after that, a woman came up to me and asked if I wanted to *buy* drugs. I said no. *What a busy night for solicitors,* I thought.

Then a man came up to me and asked if I was a working girl. Oh, I laughed. How desperate someone must be to try to buy sex from a little old lady with a walker. I should have just said no, but instead, in the flirtiest voice I have I asked, "Now what do you think?"

Another time, there was a man who didn't believe me when I told him I didn't sell sex. He asked me again and again until I actually got annoyed. He mistook my emotion for chemistry, for desire. He held out a twenty to me and asked what he could get for it. So I took the twenty and told him he would get nothing.

The man went to get the police. He actually brought an officer back with him.

"She stole from me," he told the officer.

I ogled him; I couldn't believe what a trap he was walking himself into.

"What happened?" asked the officer.

"He asked if I were a prostitute," I answered. "I told him no. He wanted to know what I'd sell him for twenty dollars. I'm not a prostitute, so I sold him nothing."

"She took my twenty!" said the man.

The officer laughed, just like I had, at this man's absurdity. Then the officer arrested him.

Once, I took a job in a police station as a janitor. I would go in the evening and sweep and dust and vacuum and mop. An acquaintance who knew I'd gone back to school as an adult made fun of me for taking that job.

"Is that what you went to school for?" they chirped at me.

I said, "Look, it's a job."

I never understood looking down on a job, especially a job like that. Surely everyone liked when public buildings were clean and well-maintained; they didn't enjoy trash and broken toilets and broken bulbs in stairways. They enjoyed walking through public buildings and ignoring all the cleanness, which is the evidence of a poorly paid person's labour.

"It's a paying job," I'd say. "Why didn't you go get it?"

I can't understand people who don't have ambition. That job had been open a long time when I took it, while people I knew would complain they couldn't find one. I found it.

Life can throw you surprises, but in a lot of ways, you get what you get; you reap what you sow. I don't understand jealousy; it is better to just see others have worked hard for what they have and to try to work hard too.

I've been ambitious even when it's hard.

It is sometimes hard to be ambitious. It is hard to look at a paper and see a flower when you are hungry and you have no home. I had friends in the street world that became very sloppy and too free, which resulted in deaths by overdose, suicide, tragic things. But what is your alternative? You're stuck. No one can get you unstuck but you.

I used to know an Aboriginal stripper. She dressed like a real squaw: everything in buckskin. She was beautiful and a compelling dancer. She was also a dedicated mother; she worked as a waitress when her three kids were at school and as a stripper when they were asleep.

Her husband would try every now and again to make her stop stripping using guilt. "What kind of mother strips while her children sleep?" he'd say. "What kind of wife leaves her husband alone to go dance for other men? How could you?"

"How can I? We have to eat." she'd scoff at him. "If you want me to stop stripping, get a job. Replace this income. I work all day and strip all night. I'd love it if you pitched in and I could take nights off. Is getting a job too hard for you?"

She kept stripping, so I suppose it was easier for him to nurse his bruised pride than to step up and contribute to his family so his wife could rest.

Again, life is hard, but some things are your own fault. He blamed his wife for dancing; he blamed the men who ogled her and blamed them for paying his bills. He never stopped to blame himself. He never saw his own part in creating the problem.

I suppose that's why I shouldn't be surprised he couldn't find a solution.

I was walking down the street once when I saw this drunken couple. They spotted me and just started hooting and hollering. The man shouted, "Are you transgender?"

I thought to myself, *Here comes trouble*, but I said, "Yes, that I am."

And they *rushed* me, raced over to me like galloping wildebeests to embrace me. They ran up so fast, so manic, I thought they were gonna attack me, you know? They were piss drunk.

Usually, I can sense the intentions of people. Usually, I can spot who is an abuser, who has been abused, who has been unscathed by either. But that pair scared me, rushing me with that alcohol-brightened spirit lighting them up like fuses of fireworks or explosives, I couldn't tell.

But they hugged me like I was a long-lost sibling, like they'd recovered something as precious as a soul.

And why were they so happy to see me, a transgender person they didn't know? I don't know. Maybe they had lost somebody like me to violence or drugs or a conservative family and I was a good reminder? I don't know. I only know it was a special moment between strangers.

IT'S THE HOPE THAT KILLS YOU

The sunsets in the place where I grew up were unlike any others I've ever known. I don't know which sunsets were more beautiful, the winter or the summer. The winter sky held all the mauves and blues and pinks. Oh, you watch that sun go down on the lake. The place we used to go to watch them was actually called the sunset lodge.

We once had a substitute teacher there, called Mrs. Smith. She had two kids, but hell if I can remember their names after all this time. But I remember they had this American accent, so different from the way we spoke in the bush.

I saw sunsets when I went home after my mother died. I only came down to my mother's funeral because one of my brothers wanted me there.

You know what? I never ever heard my dad scream or yell. I've never seen him angry. He never, ever laid a hand on any of his kids. Sometimes how gentle he was makes me wonder if he was aware of what my mother was doing. Because I never talked to him about how she treated me and some of my siblings.

I have full function. I know right from wrong. I've never, ever wanted to hurt anyone in my life, not for the sake of hurting them.

I don't even like imagining it to defend my life from someone. Some people are treated the way me and my siblings were and it turns them crazy, violent. They steal anything they want and they lash out at anyone who does anything to them, even those who try to help.

At first, I thought, *Oh, I must be like my father.* He was a peaceful man. My father never killed a moose in his life. He said he couldn't pull the trigger.

Yeah, I understand that. I guess I got that from him. He always said, "Life is life."

I said, "But you kill fish."

He said, "No, I don't; I take him out of the water. And they die. Besides, we gotta eat."

Very rationalized. I guess it seems different. And it's not like you stab the fish or something. It's more passive than shooting. It's still killing a life force, a being, because we believe in animal spirits. I don't believe in a lesser god, I guess. I believe in a higher power.

I find religion very interesting. We were savages because we worship the sun, the Creator. I said, "But your god is a giver of life. My god is the giver of life. It seems to me that we're not that primitive after all. Without the sun, nobody will survive. So he is the giver of life. Take a fish into the sun, out of the water, and the Creator kills the fish for you. The Creator lets you eat, lets you live."

I visited my father only a few times after my mother died. Space, distance, time: it all gets in the way.

I left home because it hurt too much to be there, but the distance hurt in a way too. I feel very separate from my family; some are drunks, some do drugs, some are in jail for worse things. But that distance sometimes hurts. And knowing I saw my father only a handful of times in the end of his life sometimes hurts.

Once, I took him to Montreal for a month.

My father loved Old Montreal. He spent most of his time inside the church, Notre Dame Cathédral. When we were young, my father used to always go to church. When he came to visit in Montreal, he fell in love with that church. All his life he'd gone to church quite often and I think the beauty of that church stayed with him a long time.

But after my brother Raymond was killed, my dad stopped going to church. My brother was killed by a professional trucker who was drunk behind the wheel for at least his second time. My father used to say, "How could God do this?" I didn't want him to lose his beautiful, quiet faith, so I used to tell him, "God didn't do this; a drunk driver did." I hope it helped him hold on to the good, comforting parts of his faith in God.

My brother was killed by someone who'd been rehired after his first DUI on the job. My family actually sued the company who had rehired the driver who'd caused a similar accident when drunk before.

We got money from the insurance company when we won. It gave a security net for his children and reimbursed us for the funeral. The settlement even reimbursed us for the cost of those who had to travel to Raymond's funeral. The children would have rather had their father than the settlement any day, but they were told again and again they were lucky to have those dollars, as if they were anything like having your family.

I do a lot of volunteering in Thunder Bay. I'm an Elder for Biinjitiwaabik Zaaging Anishinaabek Family Centre; I do a transgender support group and teach sewing and crafts. I also sit in on case reviews and we as elders have a monthly meeting; since the pandemic, it's done by phone.

In Rocky Bay, we do an event that's all about bringing children home. It's mostly aimed at children who were taken away, put into foster care or adopted out, or those who don't know where they've come from. We bring them home to see where they're from. They're brought by foster or adoptive parents or whomever. We have a collection of activities for them.

We bring them to Graveyard Island, to where their ancestors are buried. We do our best to point out their relations: the grandparents, great-aunts, whoever else they should know their connection to. Who they should've known growing up, who were separated from them by the pass system, residential school, the old system of adopting kids out or the modern system of taking them to out-of-community foster care. After all, history doesn't repeat, exactly, but it rhymes.

We show them the land where they should have formed their identities and grown from children to young adults to elders, like we did for thousands of years before contact with Europeans. They see the beautiful shores of Lake Nipigon and the small mountains that surround us.

For me, it always feels like a blessing to come home to Rocky Bay, if even for a day. During these events, I see some of the children realize this blessing too. They get to see what should have been home and, for a moment, it is like they've never left. Like they'd never been taken.

I just wrote a little article for our band office in Rocky Bay. I wrote about what it was like, what people were like and how they helped each other.

We did another of these events just recently. Nearly two hundred kids came. I made twelve dozen cupcakes for the event. They were truly homemade: no mix, no mixer, just my own recipe and own hands stirring. Red velvet, limoncello, chocolate martini, vanilla, carrot, and pineapple. Delicious. Made with care. Not traditional, but a taste of home all the same.

The children got to come home. This project has been very successful; there are children who had no idea where they were from who now know the names and sometimes even the faces of the families they lost.

When I left, it wasn't even a reserve yet. It wasn't yet Biinjitiwaabik Zaaging Anishinaabek, wasn't yet Rocky Bay. But just because the community didn't have a name yet didn't mean it wasn't a community; everybody looked after everybody as best they could. If your kid was out and about in the village and it was lunchtime, you knew whoever they were with would make sure they got fed. It wasn't seen as any trouble to put an extra potato and dumpling in the family soup. Everybody helped each other in the ways we knew how.

When I returned after forty years or so, it felt like the community had forgotten that. One of the first things I did when I was back was volunteer at the school. The school staff told me I was the first volunteer they could ever remember having. It made me sad. There was a reserve filled with parents and aunts and uncles and family but no one came to volunteer for the children. The children are the future. The future doesn't become better on its own; it needs support.

The reserve was so different when I went back. When I was a child, Finnish and Ukrainian loggers lived in the logging camp nearby and bought our crafts and ate at Dirty Gertie's restaurant, even when us kids were dancing there.

When I went back, there was this new racism. It was anti-white, as if the whites who came through as tourists were the same whites who built the Indian day school, who let the teachers abuse us. It was even held against the East Indians and the Asians who came to the area; they were slurred as pakis or slant-eyed or Chinamen.

I wonder if I don't notice racism in Thunder Bay now because, as a trans Anishinaabe woman, I've heard it all before and it rolls off me. But then I think back to other places I've lived. In Thunder Bay, I've never been told "We don't serve your kind here; we don't let people like you in here."

No, in Thunder Bay, what I notice—what hurts me—is the distance between some of my family and I, between me and the ones who don't accept me as trans but accept my brothers who have murdered or raped or lost themselves to drugs. I found myself and revealed myself, and that made some of my family reject me. But I found myself; I'd find myself a hundred times knowing who I am now, knowing what it cost to become the true me. I didn't lose anything.

It felt different in Rocky Bay when I went back. I had gone back for a funeral, but that wasn't the only reason it felt different. It felt like everybody was for themselves now, like if your kid were out and about and lunchtime came, whoever they were with would send them home like a burden rather than feed them.

When I was a child there, we all worked. I carried water. I helped keep the fires going. My siblings and I wove baskets and helped pick pine cones for the forestry people. Nowadays, there are adults on the reserve who have never worked a day in their life. I never can understand that. How do they expect their community to improve if they won't carry the heavy loads that build a new foundation, a new future?

Yes, it is hard to be First Nations in Canada. Yes, our people have had so much taken away and have suffered. It can be hard to find a job; people don't always want to hire First Nations, or they don't trust the work ethic of people from reserves who don't have the experience or education the employer thinks they need.

Yes, it is hard. But how do you expect anything to get better if you don't try? If you don't do the things when they're hard, how do you expect to ever learn enough to find anything easy?

I thought life didn't get much harder than mine until I went to India in my twenties. The slums there are so much different from ours. There are so many people living so densely that it's hard to imagine they have enough to go around no matter how hard they work.

I saw people there working so hard for the privilege of not having enough rather than having nothing. I saw children gathering plastic bags from the litter, gathering them to resell for reuse. I saw children searching through trash to find anything valuable. I came home and Canada felt like the land of opportunity.

It was all I could do to take advantage of my chances. I had to make the most of my chances or I would never see my dreams become real. I might not even have seen my hunger's demands met.

All my life is a dream and a fantasy. If you live a life where you're lucky at the right times, a lot of times it is your dreams and fantasies that make things happen, that reveal opportunities.

I almost died recently, in Thunder Bay, in the place I've grown to call home. Thunder Bay has grown to be the place where I've been the happiest, living and working in this little lakeside city that once seemed like an unfathomable metropolis to me.

Thunder Bay became a place where I led patient advocacy, where I worked to better the reality for women and Indigenous and trans people like me. I carved out a home here, collected all the fine china I could fit in my apartment. But recently, I almost died here.

I'm not sure how it all started, with my hernia or with my dialysis or just bad luck and age. It might have been a longstanding problem that wasn't properly fixed and one day went wrong. I'll never know for sure.

All I know is that I had a pain in my abdomen for three years that would go away if I laid down. At first it was only once a month, not often at all, so I ignored it. Then it was once or twice a week, so I mentioned it to doctors, who also ignored it. Then it was three to four times a day. One evening I woke up about eleven at night in so much pain that I couldn't move. I had to call 911.

I got so sick I was hospitalized. The same pain? I suppose I can't be sure. I'm checked on by doctors so often that you would think emergencies couldn't sneak up.

I got an infection and a part of my bowel died. It died while it was inside of me, festering and rotting and paining me while interrupting the digestion of all the strength I'd need to survive this. The doctors and nurses of Thunder Bay took me apart and cut me open and found my dead parts and removed them. I don't remember anything from the May 15 until July 14. I wish I could tell you more about nearly dying, but so much of my memory is just empty.

When they did the surgery to remove the dead bowel, they almost lost me. My heart went crazy, my blood pressure went crazy. I wonder if they could smell the dead inside of me as they cut it off. My bowel was rotting inside me; they must've been able to smell it.

Then I began to recover. I drifted through time and space while I was ill for those weeks. I lived in the ICU; I lived with tubes and pumps keeping me alive. But the ICU is not what I saw. I saw the hospital, built in two sections, divided by a river.

I could see plants growing out of the water and could see the trout swimming under the sparkling surface. I could hear birds in the trees just beyond me. The nurses would roll me from the ICU to the dialysis unit, but I didn't see the hospital. I was rolled past the flowing river into a shopping mall.

I would try to cover myself from the ogling shoppers. I was too sick to recover any dignity from these imaginary judging eyes. I was filled with tubes and couldn't move. A tube was breathing for me; a tube was feeding me. I was so embarrassed and ashamed, but there was nothing I could do. I ended up in diapers because I had tried to get to the bathroom and ended up collapsed on the floor.

A male nurse or orderly—I was too far gone to tell—he picked me up like I was nothing, like I weighed eight pounds. The nurses would change my diaper and I would try to hide from the shoppers

I was seeing. Filled with tubes, I couldn't even explain this was happening to me.

I was hallucinating, but it was so real. I felt no pain; I was too bizarre and away from myself. All the fantastic and terrifying things I was seeing were feverishly real. As much as I couldn't speak past the tubes keeping me inflated and alive, I couldn't see past my hallucination to the ICU or the renal unit. Instead I saw jungles and dance halls and tried to cover myself from nonexistent, hallucinated strangers.

I recovered, and I'm on the transplant list now. That's my only hope at more time, I think. For now, I'm treading water. I had that hernia for so long; I had the dead bowel inside of me for long enough to make me sick. But I'm treading water. Sometimes I notice how much more time I take now. Sometimes it takes me all day to mop my floor; I get tired and have to rest.

I don't want to rest. I want this book to end with a bang; I want my story to end with a bang. If I could make a little bang of sparkles and fireworks go off when you get to the back page, I would.

Sickness struck me again. A mass in my body.

It's a bad sign.

For someone like me, on dialysis and waiting for transplant, this is a disaster. I can't get a transplant if I have cancer or even a benign mass. I will be too old for a transplant by the time I beat it. Ultimately, this has changed my life forever.

It has changed my death.

When I started dialysis, I never said, "I should've done this," or, "I should've done that." I simply did the things I wanted, organized my goals and ambitions around the long hours I had to spend tethered to a life-saving machine. Sometimes I think I've done more despite being tethered to dialysis than most people do their whole lives. But now there is a sense I will run out of time and run out of things to do.

Certain songs trigger certain emotions. I'll end up sitting there just bawling away and think, *Why am I crying? I can't figure out why I'm crying, but that song must have reminded me of something in my subconscious.*

There's a lot of things that I blocked out. I go from one year to the other and not remember a year between because something happened that I blocked out. Now, when songs make me cry, I think the tears come from those missing memories.

A memory came to me recently. Being in church back home, back in Rocky Bay, all those years ago. We were a poor community; even the white loggers didn't have much money. And once, at church, the collection plate went around and came back empty. As we passed it back up, my aunt Mary started singing, "Bringing in the cheap, bringing in the cheap," to the tune of the old song about shepherds and sheep.

She was good in her own way. Of course, that's true about nearly everyone.

Memories of my family keep creeping back in at this stage of my life. Some of my earliest memories are surfacing like I'm being haunted by myself from my youth.

As a child, I really loved my cousin Gertrude. But my cousins, Gertrude, Chet, Moses, Audrey, Roxanne and two other girls, they all died from complications of dialysis, of kidney failure. And two of Gertie's kids, Ralph and Abraham, who were from a different father than the man Gertie ended up marrying, they seemed to get lucky in the genetic draw. They're still healthy today.

After all the time in the hospital, I can't handle the silence anymore. In the hospital, there's beeping and announcements and doctors speaking loudly to hard-of-hearing patients. And it used to be rowdy when I first lived in this building. There used to be so much noise it unsettled me. But I would prefer to have that noise now to soothe me to sleep like the beeping and announcements in the hospital did. What I wouldn't give for nurses' voices in the hall as they chatted, promising to rush in should I need help. Now I sleep with a fan on.

This building used to have voices ringing through the halls and the walls. But someone was murdered here and there was a meth lab that got shut down. I suppose a combination of moving those folks out and the new reputation as the murder-meth building meant rowdier folks started looking elsewhere for housing. After all, the guy who ran the lab wasn't very smart. Rowdy folks want to party, but they don't want to be blown up.

Even I'm leaving this building. As soon as I get my settlement from the government, my settlement for everything I went through in the Indian day school, I'll be moving out. I'll buy a condo or a house in my niece's name. I'll live there until I die, and she'll inherit it without the inheritance tax. I love my niece and the other nephews and nieces I have. I love them like my own children, the ones I never had.

But packing is exhausting. You never realize how many things you've accumulated until it is time to gather them all and depart. I am gathering my things. I am slowly packing up my life, getting ready to move to a new chapter that will close my life off. I don't think that chapter will be in the book.

After all, I want a real copy of it before I die. My story, it feels more real when it's written down, when I read it back. I want to read my life back; I wanted you, reader, to read it back too. So this book will stop before I do.

I try to focus on others' success stories now that I won't have a successful transplant story.

Where I work now, we had a young man come into our centre. He told us he found out recently we were his home community; he'd been taken away as a baby. We managed to find his family, and he got to meet his grandmother and even his siblings. It was such a joyous reunion, such a surprise to the family. They didn't even know his mother had had him.

It makes you wonder what the circumstances were before his birth, what tragedy his mother went through that he was taken away. She lived at home when he was born, still enough of a child that she lived with her parents. And she hid the pregnancy. And she lost the baby to the care system. The rest of the family didn't even know he was missing from their lives until he came to be reunited.

This is a good story. He found his family, found his home, was welcomed back.

But it also makes me think of how my story will end. I hope it's long after this book is published. I am missing from my family.

Many of them, they don't like that I live my life as the woman I am, and it makes us absent from each other. We won't have the reunion that that boy got to have, that his grandmother and siblings rejoiced for.

Of course, I am not missing from all of my family. Many of them love me dearly. I've made more wedding cakes than I can count, mostly for nieces, the children of my cousins. I'll leave my future home to my niece with the hope that I give her the gift of housing stability for life and that she'll never know the homelessness I knew.

But as I sit with the knowledge that I've lost my chance at a transplant, I think of what else I've lost.

I had the love of my life once, Eric, a man I miss so badly I try not to remember him too often. The heartbreak is too much to bear even after all these years. Sometimes I'll hear a song or smell an aroma, and for a moment, his presence is with me like he never left. I try not to linger in memories too much lest I should grieve him so much I lose these ghostly moments too.

I walked past a florist the other day and the aroma of the flowers brought me back to my last days in Montreal. Before I left, I made the rounds of all my favourite spots, all my favourite friends. Naturally, one of my favourite things to do was go to bingo. They have bingo everywhere, but each bingo had its own flair.

I couldn't leave without sitting in my favourite Montreal bingo hall once again. And I won a thousand dollars. It went a lot further in those days, but I still spent some frivolously. I bought one hundred dollars' worth of flowers from a street vendor. Money went so far back then that I could barely carry them all.

I was leaving soon, so they wouldn't wilt in my apartment until after I left. And I wanted them to be enjoyed for as long as they were fresh. So I carried them as I walked through the city, enjoying the aroma that drifted from them with my movements and the smiles they brought to the people I passed by.

Eventually, my meandering path brought me to this Asian restaurant I'd never been to before. But on their stoop, on a little dais of sorts, they had a big Buddha sitting in a fountain. And it was so beautiful. The water was so calming. So I approached and dropped my giant bouquet into the fountain, arranging the flowers to carpet the Buddha's seat. An old man came out from the restaurant (he'd tell me later he was a monk) and asked, "Why did you come back?"

I turned to him and said, "I've never been to this restaurant before, let alone come back."

"No," he said. "No, you had reached nirvana in your last life. Why did you come back?"

Apparently, in his tradition you reached nirvana and you didn't have to come back any more. You reached the end of the life cycles souls were meant to go through; you got to resolve, extinguish. Your life energy or your soul or whatever it is that makes you reaches peace and ends its suffering.

But he said I'd done that in my last life and come back anyway. I don't know what he saw in me. But he invited me in and we talked and had tea. And he was so interesting; he was so interested in me. We talked for ages.

And looking back now, I still ask myself, *If he was right and I had a past life where I accomplished all the spiritual and physical work I was meant to, why did I come back? Why would I have chosen a life like mine?*

But I have no real answers. All I know is, even now with all the work I've done, people I've met, people I've helped or failed or loved, I still feel a sense of incompleteness. I still cannot sit still. I'm always looking for new things to do and make and work.

I work for family services and advocate for anyone I can. Once, I sat in on a court case for a woman who only spoke Anishinaabemowin. Her translator was not saying the same things the judge was saying—he was interpreting wrongly or badly and this woman was agreeing to things she wasn't being told the truth of. So I stood up in the gallery and told the judge, "This translator is not translating right; this isn't right."

After a long investigation, the court agreed. So they investigated other cases he'd translated for and almost a hundred people's lives changed because they got new hearings or new trials and finally were heard in good translation. Is that enough to justify this life of mine? To make my work complete?

Or recently I quilted and embroidered two baby blankets and made a little doll for a pregnant friend, the daughter of one of my doctors. When I gave her the doll, she laughed.

"When I was just a child, a patient of my father's made me a doll," she said. "And now you, a patient of my father's, has made one for my child too."

Is that enough to justify this life of mine?

Or the endless wedding cakes and birthday cakes and no-special-occasion-needed pies? The dollar I have for the man looking for bus fare? Or the children whose cases I sit on at family services? What's enough? Will the thing that's enough be big or small? Is it all of the things?

Life is life. That's what my father told me once about hunting, about life: Take the fish out of the water and don't see it as killing. I feel like that fish now, taken out of water. I've lost my chance at a transplant. I'm out of the water; I have fewer ways to swim now. But I'm not a fish.

I dreamt of my father recently. It felt so real. I could see the gleam of his eyes and the ruffle of his hair and almost smell his woodsy, clean scent.

"Are you coming to get me?" I asked him.

I thought maybe his spirit felt so close because it was my time to join him, that he would be coming for me sooner than later. But he shook his head.

"One day, I will come to get you," he told me. "But not yet. No, you've got a long wait."

So I have a long wait before I find out what happens when we die.

I won't spend that time waiting idle, though. I can still create, still work, still advocate. I am bound to the dialysis chair, but I make the most of every moment outside of it. I've just bought a home. I make wedding cakes for my nieces, I work for the family care services. I am still a vibrant and protective member of my community. I worked for twelve hours just yesterday, a day full of meetings at the Rocky Bay Family Services trying to qualify more foster families for children from our community.

I'm proud of what I've done with my life. I think Eric would be too. I think he would have enjoyed seeing me become the woman I am now, travelling the world with me. I think of the home we would have had together, the beautiful cabinets he would have made me and the thousands of tiny details he would have put into making our life and home together just as beautiful.

I think of the afterlife, but I also know life goes on. It went on without Eric; it will go on without me. But I've done everything I wanted in my life. There's no feeling sorry for myself.

Some of the people I sit on dialysis with sit with that *poor me* syndrome. They don't comply with all the dialysis instructions, they eat things they shouldn't, they drink things they shouldn't. They pity themselves and forget to value themselves, to take care.

I never had that. I kept my life going when I started dialysis. I still travelled, just less. I still eat good food, just the kinds that are safe for my body. I've had hard things happen to me in my life; I've been beaten, molested, raped, homeless. It's all happened to me. So I don't pity myself; I value myself and I heal myself. I take care of myself the way I need to.

I found ways to develop trust. It was hard because some of the people who were supposed to love me are the ones who treated me the worst in this life. But I got over it. I got over it without drugs, without alcohol.

I have spoken to a lot of trans communities throughout Canada. I say to them, "You know, if you need to get stoned or get high to put on your make-up, just forget about it. Because who are you fooling? And who are you helping? It's not yourself."

I think sometimes of the trans girls I used to dance with in New York; I wish they'd been able to stay sober. I saw them lose themselves to alcohol or drugs after they fought so hard to find themselves in transition. A waste. I was always determined that my life would not be a waste.

Ages ago, I was talking to my brother, Charles, before he died. He asked me, "Are you going to start preparing for your funeral? We're getting to that age."

"No," I said. "What do I care? I'll be dead. That can be your problem."

But I joked with him that I wanted two white horses to pull my casket to the cemetery in a wooden wagon. And I wanted a mariachi band. I joked that I'd need to find someone with white horses who would bring them into town for me.

My niece said to me once, too, that I had to prepare my funeral plans. But she said I should get my baking done for the tea party after my funeral. How I laughed at the idea that because I am the family baker, I would bake even for my own funeral.

I think of myself, of the little girl I was in Rocky Bay, back home, before it stopped being home in so many ways. I never lost her, that little girl I used to be. I carried her with me through homelessness, abandonment, through all the bad in my life. She carried me through all the good. I didn't lose her to drugs or alcohol, and I didn't lose her to fatalism when I found myself on dialysis.

That little girl I used to be would be proud of me, too, and perhaps that is most important.

Printed in the USA
CPSIA information can be obtained
at www.ICGtesting.com
LVHW040837151023
761077LV00008B/30

9 780228 896418